SUCCESSFUL WRESTLING

Coaches' Guide for Teaching Basic to Advanced Skills

Art Keith, EdD
Joel E. Ferris High School
Spokane, WA

Leisure Press
Champaign, IL

Library of Congress Cataloging-in-Publication Data

Keith, Art.
   Successful wrestling : coaches' guide for teaching basic to
advanced skills / by Art Keith.
     p.   cm.
    ISBN 0-88011-329-4
    1. Wrestling--Coaching.   I. Title.
   GV1196.3.K45 1990
  796.8'12--dc20
                                                    89-12098
                                                       CIP

ISBN: 0-88011-329-4

Developmental Editor: June I. Decker, PhD
Copyeditor: Peter Nelson
Assistant Editors: Valerie Hall and Timothy Ryan
Proofreader: Wendy Nelson
Production Director: Ernie Noa
Typesetter: Brad Colson
Text Design: Keith Blomberg
Text Layout: Jayne Clampitt
Cover Design: Jack Davis
Cover Photo: Dave Black
Interior Photos: Brad Jones
Printer: Versa Press
Models: Bruce Backlund, Jason Colquhoun, Chris Hinkley, Ty Lingo, and Andy Siegrist

Printed in the United States of America

10 9 8 7 6 5 4 3 2 1

Leisure Press
A Division of Human Kinetics Publishers, Inc.
Box 5076, Champaign, IL 61825-5076
1-800-342-5457
1-800-334-3665 (in Illinois)

To Charles "Zac" Zacur, my high school wrestling coach at Canby High School, Canby, Oregon, and to all the fine coaches and wrestlers who have contributed so much to my life through wrestling.

CONTENTS

FOREWORD

There are a lot of good coaches in our country, but there aren't many who can (or are willing to) put their knowledge of the sport in writing. Art Keith has done just that. In this book he shares the philosophy and system that has made him such a successful coach.

Art was a winner in his very first coaching job and has proven himself throughout the years. I can personally vouch for Coach Keith, as he coached me through two high school state championships. I watched him develop three other high school programs and do an outstanding job as head coach at the University of Oregon. During his university reign, his teams consistently did well in the NCAA and he produced several All-Americans, including NCAA champion John Miller (118 lb).

Art understands that just knowing techniques is not enough to have a successful program. It is what you teach and when you teach it. It is knowing how to drill what you teach and knowing the proper progression of skills.

This book can be used in many different levels of wrestling, such as college coaching classes and high school, junior high, and club wrestling. Every coach should have a copy as a guide book, a reference book, and a problem solver.

I highly recommend this book to all wrestling coaches. I wish it had been written sooner. It would have saved me and many others a great deal of time.

Ron Finley
University of Oregon Coach
United States Olympic Coach

PREFACE

The quality of wrestling has improved tremendously over the last 20 years. This improvement is the result of so many fine wrestlers having become coaches, passing along their skills to their teams.

Not all successful wrestlers have become good coaches, though, nor have all truly outstanding coaches first been great wrestlers. Teaching young athletes to become championship wrestlers requires a special understanding of how to *teach* wrestling techniques, not just perform them. Successful wrestling requires a skilled performance based on a few fundamental techniques. Successful coaching of wrestling, however, requires a different set of skills.

One of the real joys of successful coaching is to watch the increasing success of beginning wrestlers as they master the fundamental skills. *Successful Wrestling* was written to help you experience that joy. Learning how to teach wrestling will, in turn, help young athletes experience success. This book provides a stairway to success. Specific techniques that should be learned by all good wrestlers are presented in order from very simple skills to more complex moves. The basic body positions and movements are presented in proper sequence. Teaching tips are shared, and common errors are identified.

Most wrestling coaching books are organized around topical areas such as takedowns, reversals, escapes, and pins. However, this book is presented overall from simple to complex, as is each technique. Emphasis is directed toward helping you learn how to teach these skills. The book also shows how to organize and direct individual and team practices.

Successful Wrestling does not include hundreds of variations or a wide variety of ''clinic moves.'' Instead, a specific program is presented for teaching wrestlers the basic skills needed to be successful. A good wrestler does not need to be skilled in hundreds of techniques.

Successful Wrestling is organized in three stages, consisting of several steps and many specific techniques organized in the sequence in which they should be taught. Basic wrestling positions on the feet and on the mat are shown first, followed by a basic move or two from each position. The earliest techniques have the common element of continuous movement in one direction, which makes the techniques easier to master and to teach. Later techniques are more complex and require a change in direction and more muscular coordination. However, the more advanced moves build on skills taught earlier.

Stage 1, ''Beginning Wrestling Skills,'' is intended for 1st-year wrestlers. The techniques included in this stage's eight steps are the basics for beginners. Older boys may accomplish these moves in less than a year; junior high wrestlers might spend 2 years learning them. Regardless of the length of time spent on Stage 1, the steps should be climbed one at a time.

The first step illustrates basic position and fundamental movements from the neutral, top, and bottom positions. Next, the double-leg tackle is shown. Step 3 shows two stand-ups for escapes; step 4 shows how to return the man to the mat after a stand-up. Controlling the down wrestler (step 5) is followed by simple pinning combinations. Stage 1 concludes with the switch as a beginning reversal and pinning from a control ride. Upon completion of these eight steps, wrestlers should possess skill in basic movements and stance, one takedown, two escapes, techniques for controlling the man on the mat or returning him to the mat, four pins, and one reversal.

Stage 2, "Intermediate Wrestling Skills," provides an extension and further development of the positions and skills learned earlier. Generally, 2nd-year wrestlers can learn these techniques. However, the highly skilled wrestler may get into some of the steps late in his 1st year, or some of the steps may be saved until the 3rd year.

The techniques in this stage require agility, a change of direction, and coordination. Takedowns are included, such as the outside fireman's carry and the single-leg attack in step 9. Step 10 shows how to ride for control and for scoring back points using the double-wrist ride, the double bar arm, the turk ride, and the inside turk. The standing switch is shown in step 11. Step 12 develops skill in three mat reversals—the duck-out, the Granby tuck roll, and the sit-out. This stage concludes with a set of takedown counters.

Stage 3, "Advanced Wrestling Skills," consists of more complex techniques. Because they build on earlier positions and techniques, they can probably be mastered only by wrestlers with 2 or 3 years of experience. A good high school wrestler or a superior junior high wrestler may be ready for some of these advanced skills earlier than the majority of the team.

Many of the moves shown are special-situation techniques. Step 15 shows more takedowns—the fireman's carry and the high-crotch single. Leg rides, including the cross-body ride, the force nelson with double-leg ride, the guillotine, and another turk ride position, are illustrated in step 16. Takedown options and specialty takedowns are demonstrated in steps 17 and 18. Coaching points that provide a basis for additional success form the last step.

A successful wrestling program based on these 19 steps will provide ample opportunity for wrestlers to become skilled in several basic techniques. Although all of the steps should be taught, wrestlers should not expect to perform all of the techniques in each position. Two good takedowns, two or three breakdowns leading to pinning situations, and two or three reversals or escapes are all that a wrestler needs for better-than-average success. As a coach, you should stress proper execution of each of the fundamentals, aggressive application of each movement, and proper selection of techniques. Many really good wrestling teams specialize in only limited groups of moves and yet experience high levels of success.

Many coaching clinics today focus on the seven basic skills that have been identified as necessary for success. These skills are discussed throughout this book. In step 1, for instance, penetration and level change are taught. Position and motion are stressed with almost every technique. Lifting moves are part of several skills. Because the author chose not to include throws in this book, the back step and the back arch are not stressed.

This book was not intended as decoration for the bookshelf. It is a working book, a practical, sequential guide to successful wrestling. The book belongs in the practice room, on the mat, where coaches and wrestlers can have ready access to the illustrations and directions.

Scan the book's contents to get a general feel for the flow of the techniques. Then examine step 19 for an analysis of how the positions and movements of the techniques are related and how they build on one another. Then start at step 1 and climb to the top of the winner's platform with *Successful Wrestling*.

ACKNOWLEDGMENTS

I would like to gratefully acknowledge and thank members of the Joel E. Ferris High School wrestling team for their help in the production of this book. The principal models were Bruce Backlund, Jason Colquhoun, and Chris Hinkley. These wrestlers used the skills they learned at Ferris and by posing for the book to win 70 matches while losing 9 during their senior year. Bruce placed second and Jason fourth in Washington for Ferris; Chris moved to Montana, where he won a state championship. Ty Lingo and Andy Siegrist also posed for some of the picture sequences; Brad Jones was our photographer. My assistant coach, Bill Saye, and members of the wrestling team gave encouragement and support.

Anna Brown expertly typed the manuscript with some assistance from Holly Sutherland. Ferris High School, Spokane, Washington, contributed the use of its wrestling room.

BEGINNING WRESTLING SKILLS

Wrestling is a highly complex sport that might seem to a newcomer like it would be hard to learn. Yet the fundamentals, as in any other sport, can be taught to persons who have average physical ability and are willing to practice. The first section of *Successful Wrestling* is designed for wrestlers just beginning the climb to the winner's platform. Eight steps are presented in the order in which they should be taught. You should begin with step 1, ''Position and Movement,'' and move slowly from there with your novice wrestlers. Gradually add steps 2 and 3 to the practice schedule.

As the practice season progresses and you teach additional steps, you should incorporate all of the earlier steps in the wrestling practice session. First, use intensive drill and massed practice when you introduce a new technique or skill. Then add the movement drills to the warm-up or conditioning phase of practice in order to provide reinforcement of the skills learned earlier.

Many of the techniques taught in this first stage use basic positions and movements that are added to in later steps. You should go slowly in teaching these basic wrestling skills. Beginners do not need to be impressed by a wide range of possibilities, but they do need to build a sense of confidence. They will win many matches with the beginning techniques shown in this first stage. Actually, a wrestler could be quite successful if he became expert only in the moves illustrated in Stage 1.

Even intermediate and advanced wrestlers should be drilled on the skills shown in this section. Between seasons, especially, they forget many important coaching points that lead to success.

Stage 1 contains eight steps that should be climbed one at a time. Basic position and movement are introduced first because of their obvious necessity. Stance and movement for the neutral, down, and top positions are illustrated along with appropriate drills. One takedown is included, the double-leg tackle. Simple escapes come next, with the inside and outside stand-ups. Step 4 shows how to take a man back to the mat from the rear standing position, where the top wrestler would be if his opponent used a stand-up.

Three methods of riding a man for control on the mat make up step 5. Simple pinning combinations come in step 6, which shows the half nelson and the bar arm. The switch is introduced as the only reversal in the first set of steps. Stage 1 ends with the cross face cradle.

When wrestlers have climbed all the steps in this first stage, they will have learned basic position and movement, two escapes, one reversal, five riding or controlling moves, and three pins. A wrestler can easily become quite skilled in this set of techniques in one season.

STEP 1

POSITION AND MOVEMENT

Most successful athletes recognize the essential requirements of proper body position and correct movement principles for their sports. Successful wrestlers are no exception. Whenever a good wrestler or a good coach begins to describe a particular skill, he begins with a demonstration and explanation of body position. He tells of the importance of correct placement of hands, feet, and head. He stresses a low center of gravity and correct body posture.

He also describes the movement of body parts. He stresses relaxed but explosive movements. He mentions basic movement principles such as "shoulders and head up," "hips low and coiled," or "extend the hand and post it."

The basic positions and movements illustrated in this first step toward successful wrestling form the foundation for all the other techniques in this book. Early in a wrestler's career, he should become skilled in these fundamentals. He should be reminded of the importance of the basics as he learns additional skills. Even the experienced wrestler is careful about having the right position because he knows that success comes from continually doing the little things correctly.

Successful wrestlers are comfortable yet poised for action in the three basic starting positions—neutral, down, and top. You should drill your wrestlers on position as they learn where each part of the body should be. Sometimes you should show bad position so that your wrestlers recognize the difference between correct and incorrect placement of hands, feet, and other body parts.

You need to teach your wrestlers to move their bodies as a coordinated unit as they learn technique. Drills that emphasize the basic movements and maintain the proper body position are the most important aspect of teaching beginners how to wrestle. Position must be maintained throughout the execution of a move. All parts of the body function as a whole in attack, defense, or counterattack. Placement of head, hands, knees, and feet affects the direction and speed of motion by the body.

NEUTRAL OR STANDING STANCE

Successful takedown technique is dependent upon proper movement. A good stance is required to give the wrestler the base from which to attack or counterattack his opponent. Because aggressive action is required to secure the takedown, the stance illustrated in this section is an attacking stance. The wrestler is coiled and posed to penetrate deeply as he launches his takedown moves.

Two basic stances are used by wrestlers: a square stance and a staggered stance. Although both of these are popular, all the takedown techniques, basic leg attacks, and counters in this book begin from the staggered stance. Young or inexperienced wrestlers can use it more easily. An added advantage is that the drive foot is already planted to provide the necessary forward momentum in leg attacks.

Staggered Stance

The wrestler has his weight evenly distributed on the balls of his feet. The head is upright, the knees are bent, and the right foot is forward but under the shoulders. The left foot is firmly planted under the hips; the toe is turned out at almost a 90° angle so that the inside of the foot becomes the driving surface. The hands are in front with palms down; the hand position keeps the wrestler's weight forward (Figure 1.1). From this stance the wrestler can drive forward off the planted back foot (Figure 1.2) or can execute a drop step (Figure 1.3). In either case, the wrestler uses the back leg as a driving force while starting his forward movement with a small jab step with the front foot.

Figure 1.1. Staggered stance.

Figure 1.2. Drive step.

Figure 1.3. Drop step.

Penetration and Level Change

The drive step and the drop step are each coupled with a lowering of the hips, or level change, and penetration with the right knee. Figure 1.4 shows this as it would be executed for a double-leg takedown.

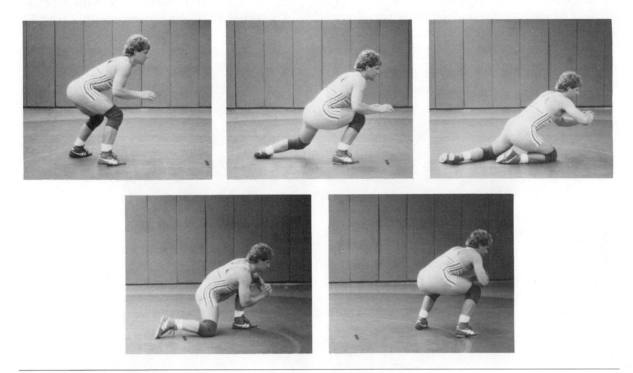

Figure 1.4. Penetration and level change.

The emphasis in the penetrating motion should be on dropping the hips while extending the lead knee. A distance of about 3 feet should be traveled by the hips and shoulders. Because the opponent will probably sprawl to counter, the wrestler should penetrate *beyond* the opponent's starting position.

Incorrect body position is shown in Figure 1.5, with the head down, and in Figure 1.6, where the lead knee is not flexed and the hips are not lowered. Not only is this latter position hard on the knee because of the angle of force, but the penetration is not deep enough.

Figure 1.5. Incorrect penetration position with head down.

Figure 1.6. Incorrect penetration position with knee not flexed.

Movement

Wrestlers need to learn to move in the staggered stance with comfort and in all directions. Wrestlers may merely pivot around the front foot, going right or left (Figure 1.7); or they may move sideways (Figure 1.8) or forward and back. The sideways and front-and-back movements are done with small steps while maintaining good position. At no time should the wrestler cross his feet or get them too close together. Sometimes a wrestler will need to protect his lead leg against attack with a quick pivot motion (Figure 1.9).

Figure 1.7. Pivot.

Figure 1.8. Movement sideways.

Inside Control

Another important part of the standing stance is the use of the hands to gain inside position and control. The only reason for tying up is to be able to move the opponent around in order to set up a takedown. Thus, when a wrestler ties up with his opponent, he should do so firmly

Figure 1.9. Quick pivot.

and assert his control. The inside hand position gives the best control. In addition, the man who has his hands on the inside is better able to shoot under for a leg tackle. Figure 1.10 shows Wrestler A (on the left) establishing inside control. At the same time, he blocks attempts by Wrestler B to tie up.

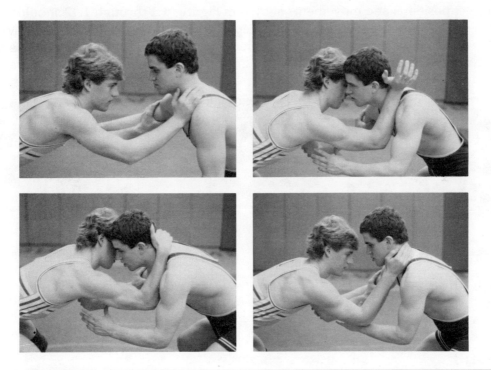

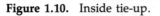

Figure 1.10. Inside tie-up.

Wrestler A raises his hands up and inside B's forearms. He grasps B's right arm above the elbow with the left hand. This action blocks B's attempts to tie (and also sets up techniques to be illustrated later). A's right wrist is planted against B's collarbone; his elbow is down to block penetration by B. A cups his hand behind B's head with a quick tug. This action usually causes B to react back against pressure. A can then shoot under for a leg tackle. B tries to force his left hand inside A's elbow. By rotating the elbow to the inside, A blocks B's attempts at inside control.

Often the wrestler reaches for the tie-up from the outside and gives his opponent inside position and control. Figure 1.11 shows this incorrect technique by the wrestler on the left.

Figure 1.11.   Incorrect inside tie-up.

The importance of the inside tie-up and the resulting control will be illustrated many times in this book. Drills such as the Tie-Up and Release Drill will help wrestlers automatically tie up correctly. Wrestlers should tie up from the inside out for most effective control. You should have wrestlers face each other in the proper stance and drill, establishing inside control, shown in Figure 1.12.

The correct positions and movements shown in Figures 1.1 through 1.12 should be practiced many times. You should drill wrestlers one step at a time and on your command. More experienced wrestlers should also be drilled on these movements, but the action can be speeded up, or the wrestlers can independently go through the movements solo or with a partner.

Figure 1.12.   Tie-up and release drill.

Team Drill

Figure 1.13 shows a team drill using the drive step for penetration and emphasizing both movement and position. You can have the entire team form lines to practice moving across the mat with this drill.

DOWN STANCE AND MOVEMENT

The primary consideration for securing reversals and escapes is to establish a sound base, or platform, from which to operate. Failure to have a good base leads to unsuccessful moves at the best and to giving up near falls at the worst. The proper down stance is one which has most

Figure 1.13. Team drive step drill.

Figure 1.14. Groin stretching exercises.

of the weight back over the hips with the head and shoulders up. This position is usually quite difficult to teach. The position is not difficult; it just does not seem to be a natural one. Teach your wrestlers the importance of using their legs and backs instead of their arms.

The most important thing for the wrestler to remember when working to establish a good base is to keep the center of gravity low and the arm and leg braces spread wide. Both of these requirements can be met with concentrated practice and effort. A high degree of hip and leg flexibility is necessary to keep the braces wide and the center of gravity low. Exercises to teach this flexibility are shown in Figure 1.14.

The stance in Figure 1.15 shows a low center of gravity, with most of the weight over the hip and leg area. Some wrestlers prefer the toe-tucked-under position because they think it gives them more mobility and quickness. The advantage of the toe-extended position, though, is that it prevents ankle rides.

The four-point stance shown in Figure 1.16 is unstable and has a high center of gravity. Too much weight is forward on the hands. A wrestler can be easily controlled in this position.

Figure 1.15. Correct down stance.

Figure 1.16. Incorrect down stance.

Knee Scoot

One simple movement that should be learned early in a wrestler's quest for success is the knee scoot, shown in Figure 1.17. The knee scoot helps the wrestler establish a position to hand-fight. It also emphasizes the importance of a low center of gravity and of forward motion, keeping the weight centered over the hips and legs. Many escapes and reversals can be executed from this position; therefore, wrestlers should work to perfect this technique.

From the position shown in the last photo of Figure 1.17, the wrestler executes a reversal or escape move. If his opponent drives him forward, he may be forced down into a stance with weight on his hands. He must then scoot his knee or knees forward and repeat the lifting action of the shoulders.

Figure 1.17. Knee scoot.

Return to Base

The next movement drill is designed to prevent one of the biggest mistakes that the down wrestler can make. Often he gets stopped when he starts a move for an escape or reversal. He must

Figure 1.18. Correct return to base.

then return to his base with his hips in the air and get his knees back under him. If he straightens out one or both of his legs, he will end up on his stomach in a very bad defensive position.

The correct movement and return to base is shown in Figure 1.18. The wrestler has a proper down position. He starts a short sit-through with his left leg and drops (or is forced by his opponent) to the mat on his left shoulder. The wrestler steps around hard and low with his right leg as he pivots with his hips up; the left leg stays tucked under as a pivot support. By scooting his knees forward, the wrestler returns to a good down stance with a low center of gravity and with head and shoulders up.

The difference between the correct and the incorrect (Figure 1.19) return to base is in the coiled bottom leg. By correctly keeping the knee tucked under and pivoting the hips up over it, the wrestler maintains a base for additional movements. If he straightens the bottom leg, though, he has no brace to elevate his hips and no power because of the extended position. In the incorrect position illustrated, the wrestler straightens his inside leg as he turns to his stomach.

Figure 1.19.   Incorrect return to base.

Up From Flat

Often a wrestler gets broken down from his hands and knees and ends up in a position flat on his stomach. From this position he needs to get back to his base on his hands and knees; his opponent will try to keep him flat. Figures 1.20 and 1.21 show the correct way to get up from flat without and with an opponent, respectively. The bottom man keeps his chest low, pushes back with his hands, and forces his hips up first.

The mistake most beginning wrestlers make in trying to get up is to use their arms, which are relatively weak, rather than their legs. The wrestler should not try to do a push-up or raise his head to get back to his base on hands and knees. The simple drill illustrated in the preceding two figures teaches how to get up to the base using leg strength and hip rotation.

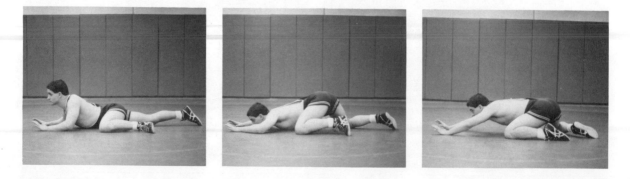

Figure 1.20.   Up from flat without a partner.

Figure 1.21. Up from flat with a partner.

Hip Heist

A more difficult movement drill, the hip heist, is illustrated in Figure 1.22. This is not so much a technique for reversal or an escape, as a movement drill to teach the basic scissoring motion of the hips and the concept of posting the weight alternately on hands, then feet. This drill teaches agility and change of direction.

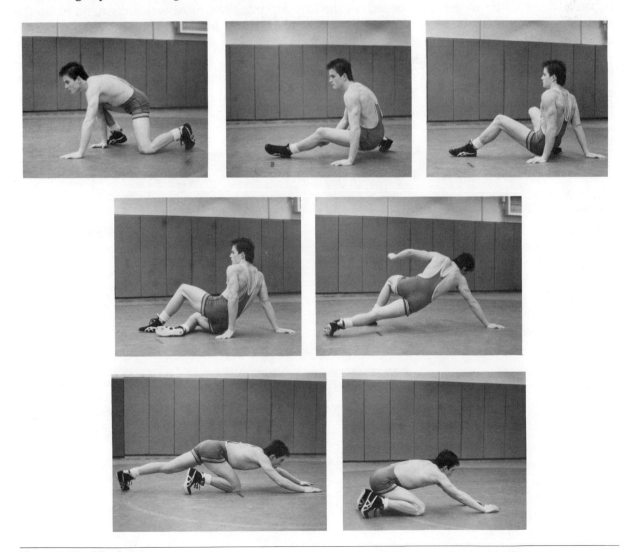

Figure 1.22. Hip heist.

From a beginning stance with toes tucked under, the wrestler hops forward by moving his left hand and right foot. His weight is on these two points as he raises his hips and projects his body forward. He sits through with his left leg; his hips do not touch the mat. He continues to shift his weight forward while starting a twisting action with his hips; he posts his right hand back for support as he continues the hip rotation. As the wrestler scissors his right leg back under his left, his weight is supported by his right arm and his left leg. As the right leg is extended through in the scissors motion, the wrestler drives off the right arm to keep his movement going across the mat. The wrestler squares up with his stomach to the mat; he pushes off both hands as he gets his knees under his hips. He completes the hip heist by pushing back with the heels of his hands and ends up in a good stance facing the opposite direction.

The hip heist motion should carry the wrestler from one edge of the circle to the other. Momentum is achieved by pushing with the heels of the hands and by extending the right leg vigorously back under the left. The hip should never touch the mat in this movement. Later in the book, techniques will be introduced that use the scissors motion and the arm posting action.

Proper Position

The wrestler needs to keep his hips as low to the mat as possible. He can accomplish this by spreading his knees; his hand and elbow position are also important. All these are shown in Figure 1.23. In order to get legs spread for the low hip position, most wrestlers need to do the stretching exercises shown earlier (Figure 1.14). Stretching the groin should be part of the warm-up activities for every practice.

As you demonstrate techniques to a group of wrestlers, they usually sit on the mat. In order to help wrestlers learn this down position, though, you should have them assume the low-hip-spread position while receiving instruction. They will be more attentive and will get added stance practice in the listening position shown in Figure 1.24.

Figure 1.23. Head, elbow, and knee positions.

Figure 1.24. Listening position.

TOP STANCE AND MOVEMENT

Maintaining control from the top position is an important skill in wrestling. Unless the wrestler learns to stay on top, he will have little success in winning matches. The wrestler must adopt an attitude of confidence about his ability to ride, or control from the top position.

Two basic goals are desired in the top position. One is to keep the opponent under control, preventing his escape or reversal. The other goal is to break a man down to the mat and turn him over for a pin. These goals are complementary; the skills that lead to the fulfillment of one goal also assist in achieving the other.

A fundamental error made by many wrestlers is to try to ride by hanging on tightly and restricting the movement of the opponent. Although this technique works part of the time, it is not the most satisfactory method of control; once the bottom man frees himself from the hold, he is free to move for an escape or reversal.

The best riding philosophy has the top wrestler restrict some of the bottom man's movement and maintain a covering position. The top man tries to flow with the other man's movement and control him by keeping him off balance and without effective braces. The following techniques identify the principles of position, restricted movement, and covering.

In Figure 1.25, Wrestler A has taken the proper starting position on top: his head is on the midline, his hands are in proper position, and his hips are tucked in close behind B. He moves into a close following position behind B. His hands are low and inside; his hips are tucked into B's rear.

From this position the top wrestler can grasp either of the bottom man's arms to restrict its movement. His forearms are low and close to the hips so he can restrict leg movements by the defensive wrestler. The area that needs to be controlled is the hips; he has the man tucked into his lap so control of the hips is easier. If the bottom man stands up, the top man is in position to go up with him and maintain control.

Figure 1.25. Top stance.

Following Down Man

The movements needed to maintain the top following position are shown in Figure 1.26. Wrestler B, on the bottom, starts a sit-through movement. A begins to follow with hands inside and hips close. As B moves into sitting position, A has kept his head up and behind B; he has his hands inside B's arms and his hips close behind. B drops his shoulder to rotate away from A, but A keeps his head above his opponent, covers the hips, and hooks with his forearms to restrict B's turning motion. As B rotates up to his base, A has followed him and still has position, with his hips tucked in close and hands inside.

Figure 1.26.   Following down man.

You should have your wrestlers drill daily in following the down man because of its importance in maintaining position. The top man always tries to keep the bottom man "in his lap," with hips pressed close. The hip area is controlled by keeping forearms inside and hooked. The top man must use his feet and legs to keep driving his hips in close behind the bottom man. The elbows are used to restrict the opponent's movement and to block his braces.

A good conditioning drill to use in the middle or near the end of a practice session is to have the bottom man put together a series of escape or reversal mat moves while the top man follows without using his hands. The top man practices hip position and glides along behind the defensive man's movement. This drill is best done in groups of three—one man down, one on top, and one resting. After 15 to 30 seconds of continuous gliding motion, the positions are rotated.

STEP 2

DOUBLE-LEG TACKLE

The double-leg tackle is an effective takedown against even the best wrestlers. It is not a difficult hold to teach beginning wrestlers if you carefully and diligently drill them on the fundamentals. Because the double-leg tackle offers so many opportunities for variation, it is a fundamental skill that every good wrestler should know.

With the drills shown in this step, wrestlers should learn to execute a good double-leg tackle. Little coordination is required in learning this technique. Only limited change of direction is needed, with most of the motion straight in.

Figure 2.1 shows the complete move executed against an opponent. Demonstrate the complete maneuver to create the mental image of the movement a wrestler will strive for in his practice of the double-leg tackle. The proper beginning stance on the feet was illustrated in step 1. Penetration and level change were also shown as part of the movement drills for the standing position. These fundamental skills should be reviewed and practiced because a successful double-leg tackle depends upon them.

Wrestler A (on the left) has inside control in the tie-up and is in a right-foot-forward staggered stance. He lifts B's right arm and takes a short step (about 8 inches) forward with his lead foot.

Figure 2.1. Double leg tackle.

He snaps his head under B's arm while changing levels with his hips. He drives his right knee between B's legs, dropping his hips low and under his shoulders and hitting B's thighs with the front of the right shoulder. A grasps B just under the singlet. He steps forward with his left foot as he begins a lifting pivot. His right ear is on B's hip as he drives with his head into B and pivots on his knee, swinging his trailing (right) foot clockwise. He continues lifting and spinning out from under B. A completes the double-leg tackle and begins to move closer into a good riding position.

The successful double-leg tackle is a combination of several separate moves. Each of these moves should be practiced as drills. These drills can be done by individuals or pairs. Some of the drills can be done with little direct supervision; others should be done in a controlled large group manner. With inexperienced wrestlers, most of the drills should be done on command as a group activity. The penetration and level change drills illustrated in step 1, under "Neutral or Standing Stance," should also be practiced as part of the double-leg tackle technique.

HEAD HOOK

The head hook movement shown in Figure 2.2 is a part of the technique that needs to be perfected through drilling. Wrestler A (on the right) bumps B's right elbow up, drops his hips forward, and begins his penetration. He shoots his head up under B's upper arm, near the shoulder. He hooks the back of his head into B's arm by tilting his head up vigorously. He has started a pivoting motion with his hips. A completes the underarm motion by stepping around and into the side of B's body. A tries to get hip contact as he pivots.

The movement illustrated in Figure 2.2 resembles one form of a duck-under (an effective takedown technique shown later). The Head Hook Drill is important for proper execution of the double-leg tackle. If the attacking wrestler does not get under the defensive man's arm, he will be blocked out of the deep penetration needed for a successful tackle.

Figure 2.2. Head hook drill.

LIFT AND SPIN

Another part of the double-leg tackle technique that needs drill work is the lift and spin. Drills on variations of this move are shown in Figures 2.3, 2.4, and 2.5.

The Lift and Sprawl Drill should be part of the normal warm-up activities for each practice session. The drill should be done on each shoulder; the left shoulder is drilled in the pictures.

The Lift and Sprawl Drill brings increased lower back lifting power. During the drill the wrestler should maintain a good stance with legs and hips, and good position with the head, hands, and shoulders. When Athlete A is weak or very inexperienced, Wrestler B can assist by hopping up into A as A starts the lift. As A gets stronger, less help is given by B. He does not resist in this drill, but he can increase the leg thrust backward in the sprawl in order to force A to lift farther and from a lower stance.

This drill should be done approximately 8 to 10 times per shoulder. The drill is best done on your verbal command at the rate of 1 lift and 1 sprawl per 2 seconds.

Figure 2.3. Lift and sprawl drill.

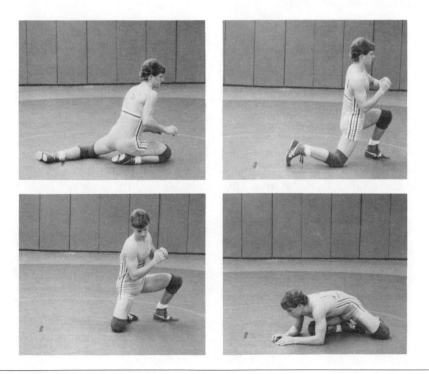

Figure 2.4. Lift and spin without partner drill.

The Lift and Spin Drill should be repeated several times without an opponent (Figure 2.4). The drill is then repeated with a passive partner, as shown in Figure 2.5. Emphasis should be placed on the head snap and on the spinning out from under. This drill does not require a lot of physical power but relies on body position and movement. Wrestlers should learn to do their drills from either side. The left shoulder motion is shown here.

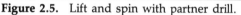

Figure 2.5. Lift and spin with partner drill.

PENETRATE

The Penetrate and Pick-Up Drill and the Knee Crawl Partner Drill (Figures 2.6 and 2.7) should be added as your wrestlers become more experienced. These drills require more strength and agility. They are, however, excellent beginning practice in lifting an opponent from the mat, in sensing body position, and in penetrating the defense of the opponent.

In the Shoulder Pop Drills (Figures 2.8 and 2.9), you should emphasize contact with the upper chest to increase the chance that the attacking wrestler will hit with his head up. The reaching

Figure 2.6. Penetrate and pick-up drill.

Figure 2.7. Knee crawl partner drill.

Figure 2.8. Shoulder pop partner drill.

action of the arms is exaggerated to enhance the shoulder penetration. This drill may be practiced with a partner, or individually on the Adam Takedown Machine™. The advantage of the solo drill with the machine is that many repetitions can be done in a very short time.

Figure 2.9. Shoulder pop machine drill.

STEP 3

STAND-UPS FOR ESCAPE

Escapes are an important part of wrestling. Often they can be gained more easily than reversals. Technique training for escapes starts with a sound, well-balanced base. Escapes are executed from this base with aggressive, explosive moves whenever possible. Sometimes, however, a wrestler needs to slowly and methodically work his way free for just a single point.

The knee scoot illustrated in Figure 1.17 provides one of the fundamental motions required to successfully execute a stand-up. The wrestler must get his knees forward and under his hips to provide the explosive force required. The position of the hands, elbows, and knees shown in Figure 1.23 provides a stance that helps in the stand-up. Flexed elbows provide a coiled position from which to launch the head and shoulders up and back.

A wrestler can execute a stand-up with either the inside leg or the outside leg; once on his feet, he can heist either left or right. So, although this step illustrates only one basic technique, the two variables create the equivalent of four different techniques.

The basic difference between the inside-leg stand-up and the outside-leg stand-up is in the foot that the down wrestler stands up with. There are many similarities between the two moves. Each stand-up requires the head and shoulders to come up and back into the top man; each requires a standing hip heist motion to clear for the escape. The choice of one over the other is probably not based on one's being better than the other. Some wrestlers simply prefer to pop up with the inside foot; others prefer to move the outside foot first.

INSIDE-LEG STAND-UP

The inside-leg stand-up (Figure 3.1) is an aggressive move initiated by the bottom wrestler from the referee's position on the mat. As the wrestler learns the movements of this stand-up escape, he will recognize the many opportunities to begin the escape technique from other positions as well, such as from an unsuccessful reversal.

The bottom wrestler (A) has his elbows out a little, and his arms are flexed to provide a good upward thrust of his upper body. He pops his inside foot up and turns his hips into B. A grips B's hand to neutralize it; he blocks B's left hand with his left elbow as he forces his hips back into B, all while coming to a good standing position. He completes the move by dropping his right hip and shoulder while popping his right leg and arm back through, as he takes a good standing stance, ready to attack for a takedown.

The success of the inside-leg stand-up depends upon a powerful thrust up with the head and shoulders. The inside leg must pop up quickly as the hips turn back into the opponent. At all times during the move, the escaping wrestler must force his hips back into the top man. The bottom man must not let his head and shoulders stay down; such an incorrect position is shown in Figure 3.2.

Figure 3.1. Inside leg stand-up.

Figure 3.2. Incorrect position for inside leg stand-up.

Cage Fight Drill

A successful inside-leg stand-up should always be followed with the bottom wrestler's anticipating the need to hand-fight for freedom. The hand-fighting techniques can be drilled separately from the stand-up, as shown in Figure 3.3. This drill is begun in a standing position. Later emphasis must be on the combined upward twisting motion of the stand-up and protective hand fighting. This drill is called the Cage Fight because the defensive wrestler (A) imagines the front part of his body as a cage into which he does not want B's hands to enter. Wrestlers should start this drill on your command and should hand fight about 4 to 6 seconds.

Figure 3.3. Cage fight drill.

Hip Motion

An additional skill that the escaping wrestler needs to learn is hip motion. By alternately thrusting his hips to the left and right, the defensive wrestler creates distance between his hips and those of the controlling wrestler. This hip motion is similar to the hip heist (Figure 1.22) and includes a change of direction. The arms are quickly driven down between the two wrestlers as the hips are turned (Figure 3.4).

Figure 3.4.   Side motion drill for hip action.

OUTSIDE-LEG STAND-UP

The outside-leg stand-up is an explosive move from the bottom designed to earn an escape (Figure 3.5). The bottom wrestler (A) must take a position with his weight back over his legs. His arms are flexed at the elbows so that he can drive his head and shoulders up and back.

The bottom wrestler is in good starting position, coiled and ready to explode. In simultaneous action, he throws his shoulders up and back while popping up to a tripod with his outside leg. He tucks his left elbow in and covers B's right hand. He forces his shoulders back and pops his inside leg up so that he is standing. He keeps his hips low and covers B's right hand with both of his. He forces B's hand down and back as he twists his trunk down to his right. He blocks B's left arm with his upper arm. With hip heist motion, A jams his arm back between their bodies, and by pivoting on his left foot, he gains a neutral position and an escape.

The outside-leg stand-up does not have to be started from the referee's position on the whistle. The bottom wrestler can keep a good base and cover the hands before starting the explosive stand-up effort. A wrestler who continuously elevates his shoulders, keeps his weight centered back over his hips, and pops his feet out in front as a brace will be very difficult to keep on the mat. The knee scoot technique (Figure 1.17) puts a wrestler in a position to execute a stand-up. Once on his feet, the bottom wrestler must keep from getting his hands and arms tied up as illustrated in the Cage Fight Drill (Figure 3.3).

Figure 3.5. Outside leg stand-up, heist right.

Hand Cover and Hip Motion Drill

Sometimes a wrestler has good success getting to his feet, but then has difficulty with the heist because he has not drilled sufficiently on the hip movement. A simple drill to improve this portion of the skill is to start wrestlers on their feet. The bottom (or front) man practices moving his hips to the left and to the right and finishes with a heist motion. The Hand Cover and Hip Motion Drill (Figure 3.6) shows the hip motion in a position where the bottom man does not have his head and shoulders up. Because he has controlled his opponent's hands and is using good hip motion and change of direction, he is still able to complete the heist and successfully score an escape.

Figure 3.6. Hand cover and hip motion drill.

The stand-up escape is a good technique to teach young wrestlers. The head and shoulders up position helps your wrestlers keep from being controlled on the mat. The hand-fighting helps them learn the principle of being aggressive on the bottom. Control of the top wrestler's hands is an effective first move for other escape and reversal techniques. The heist motion required to complete the escape is built upon the hip scissors action taught in step 1 under "Down Stance and Movement." The hip heist motion is a fundamental action needed for the switch and other moves to be taught later.

STEP 4

RETURNING A STANDING MAN TO THE MAT

Wrestling is a continuous contest, with each wrestler trying to block or counter his opponent's moves while trying to execute moves of his own. If the bottom man is good at getting to his feet, the top man must learn to control him and return him to the mat. There are several ways to return the man to the mat after he has stood up. A few important techniques will be shown here; more advanced movements requiring change of direction and better coordination will be illustrated later.

FORWARD TRIP

When the bottom man gets to his feet, the top wrestler must aggressively control him and return him to the mat. Although several techniques can be used to take a man down from the position behind, the forward trip (Figure 4.1) is the most reliable. When properly done, the defensive

Figure 4.1. Forward trip.

wrestler has practically no counter. The forward trip should result in a good riding position because the defensive wrestler ends up in an extended position on his stomach.

The bottom wrestler (B, on the left) has come to his feet with an inside stand-up. The top wrestler (A) locks his hands around B. A keeps his hips tight to B and steps his left foot in front of and inside B's left foot. He forces his left knee into B's knee and turns his hips into the thigh area while keeping a snug grip around B's waist. A's continuous pressure in and forward with his knee, thigh, and hips trips B to the mat. As they land on the mat, A posts his left arm to avoid going down under B, drives his hips into B, and prepares to shift into a riding or pinning combination.

Hips in Tight

Many situations occur in wrestling where one wrestler is in a standing position behind and must control the defensive wrestler. The best control for the top man can be secured with his hips in tight (Figure 4.2). This principle (illustrated earlier down on the mat in Figure 1.25) involves trying to keep the bottom man "in your lap." This position restricts the motion of the bottom man's hips. It also makes hand-fighting less effective. The tight follow with the hips is also necessary to get close enough to step around for the blocking or tripping action of the left leg.

Figure 4.2. Hips in tight.

Hip Crush

In the hip crush (Figure 4.3), a variation of the forward trip, the wrestler in the rear standing position forces down and forward with his elbow. If he blocks his opponent's leg and puts enough pressure on the hip, he will force the man back to the mat.

Heel Block

This slightly more advanced move can be executed from the same rear standing position. Instead of tripping forward, the top man (A) trips his opponent to the side (Figure 4.4). The top man should not pull the man down on top of himself, but he must drive his opponent across the heel block. He pops his right foot into B's right heel and drives his left knee between B's legs as he forces him over the heel block. The motion is to the side.

Figure 4.3. Hip crush.

Figure 4.4. Heel block.

LIFTS

There are two lifts that beginners can use to return a man to the mat. Both the side lift and the rear lift work well.

Side Lift

The side lift is an easy move for young wrestlers to learn. They discover that lifting a man from the mat gives them excellent control. At the same time, they learn the value of position for

for maximum lift with minimum effort. The side lift does require lifting strength, but it also teaches the principle of getting the hips in tight to lift with the legs. This lifting action is similar to the penetrate and pick-up (Figure 2.6). The hips in and the leg motion give a great deal of power.

In the side lift (Figure 4.5), the top wrestler (A) starts in a rear standing position with his hips in tight and low. He has a palm-to-palm grip with his left palm up. He forces down and back with his left elbow against B's hip to restrict B's movement. A steps around to the side, planting his hips in tight against B's thigh; he shifts his hands to a grip on B's far side. By thrusting up and in with his hips, A lifts B from the mat. He steps forward with his left foot to trap B's hips in the air while driving his shoulder forward and down, and covers B on the mat.

Figure 4.5. Side lift.

Rear Lift

The rear lift (Figure 4.6) is really a variation of the side lift. More power and control is possible from the side lift position, but sometimes the rear lift can be used effectively. Young wrestlers may find the rear lift easier because they don't have to shift position.

Figure 4.6. Rear lift.

COACHING TIPS

Although better control can be maintained in a side rear position with the rear palm up, the really important coaching point for the rear standing position is the hips-in-tight position. Sometimes it is possible to follow and control a man without a good waist lock as long as the top man has his hips in under and tight. This position takes away most of the defensive man's options.

These techniques for returning a standing man to the mat are good follow-ups to the previous step, which taught the stand-up escapes. Drills can be combined for the two techniques. In Figure 3.3, the Cage Fight, the emphasis was on the bottom man's efforts to free his hands; in Figures 3.4 through 3.6, a variety of techniques for getting the escape while in a standing position were shown. These drills can be alternated with drills for the forward trip and the side or rear lift. You can put your wrestlers in the standing position similar to the starting position in the Cage Fight Drill. You can blow the whistle to start half- or full-speed short drills, the bottom wrestler trying to control hands and heist while the top man tries to lock hands and get his hips in tight.

STEP 5

CONTROLLING
THE DOWN WRESTLER

Maintaining control from the top position is an important skill in wrestling. Unless the wrestler learns to stay on top, he will have little success. You should teach techniques for controlling the down wrestler and help your wrestlers develop an attitude of confidence about their ability to ride.

Two basic goals are part of this skill. One is to break the man down from his knees to a position on his stomach. The other goal is to control him once he is down and prevent him from regaining position on his hands and knees. These goals are complementary, and the skills leading to the fulfillment of one goal also assist in achieving the other.

This fifth step begins with illustrations of two simple breakdowns—the ankle-waist breakdown and the near-arm crotch-pry. Both of these can be easily taught to young wrestlers because not much coordination or change of position is necessary. The techniques for keeping a man broken down are important in that they lead to the next steps of pinning the opponent. The riding flat man skills emphasize the importance of the hips and a covering position for maximum control.

ANKLE-WAIST BREAKDOWN

One of the simplest breakdowns, yet one that is very effective, is the ankle-waist. This technique requires little coordination by the top man. It is effective against most first moves by the defensive man as he tries to escape or reverse. In order to have maximum effectiveness, this move should be done quickly on the start. It can be used to ride or control the bottom man. It also can lead to a breakdown to the stomach, where other techniques can be used for pinning combinations.

Far Ankle-Waist

From the top position, Wrestler A drops his left hand from the elbow to B's waist; with his right hand, A quickly grasps B's far (right) ankle while dropping his right knee in close (Figure 5.1). With a driving action of his right leg and hips, he lifts B's ankle up and forward, using his chest and left arm for additional driving action. After driving B to a flat position on the mat, he releases the ankle and covers B with both legs. He clamps his knees in and exerts hip pressure. The forward motion of A is a combination of lifting the far ankle and driving down and forward with the upper body.

Figure 5.1. Far ankle-waist.

Near Ankle-Waist

A similar breakdown is shown in Figure 5.2. The top man now shifts to the far side and grasps his opponent's left ankle. The near ankle-waist breakdown is then completed by driving forward and down.

Figure 5.2. Near ankle-waist.

The shift of weight on the near ankle-waist breakdown is necessary to achieve proper body position for the lifting and driving action. The pressure of each of the ankle rides is achieved by tilting the opponent up and forward onto his hands. The top wrestler must, however, keep a tight hold on his opponent's waist and must drive down and forward with his chest and upper body.

NEAR-ARM CROTCH-PRY BREAKDOWN

The top wrestler does not need a change of position with his body to execute the near-arm crotch-pry breakdown. The move involves his starting in a good top stance and staying in close with his hips. The importance of the position and the use of the elbows to hook and control was shown in Figure 1.26. Now specific placement and force of the arms is used to break the man down to a position on the mat.

From the standard starting position, A drops his right arm deep into B's crotch area (Figure 5.3). He turns his thumb out and extends his right arm down. He exerts a great deal of downward pressure with his elbow and upper arm across B's lower-rib and kidney area. He catches B at the elbow with his left (near) arm, then snaps his elbow down and in with a sudden aggressive movement to buckle B's left elbow in toward his body. The combined pressure of the crotch-pry up and the near elbow tucked down forces B's near shoulder to the mat. A has his right thigh tucked tightly into B's buttocks. A forces down with his hips and arches his back as he flattens B to the mat.

From the position shown in Figure 5.3, A should cover B's lower body with his legs and go into the technique for riding a flat man, which is discussed later in this step. The key to success in the near-arm crotch-pry technique is to exert quick, aggressive pressure in the proper direction with the hands and arms and with the knee from behind (Figure 5.4). The bottom wrestler is tucked into the lap of the top wrestler for maximum control.

Figure 5.3.   Near-arm crotch-pry.

Figure 5.4. Elbow pressure and knee in crease.

Control Arm

After breaking B to the mat, the top man needs to establish control that can lead to a pin. Figure 5.5 shows the top man changing sides; he is now in position for a half nelson pin (described in step 6).

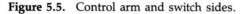

Figure 5.5. Control arm and switch sides.

The hardest part of the near-arm crotch-pry breakdown is in executing the sharp down-and-in snap of the left elbow. An alternative, which may be easier to teach beginners, is to have the top wrestler grasp the bottom elbow with a tight grip and just force the elbow down and back (Figure 5.6).

Although this elbow grip does not have the leverage that the elbow snap does, it does not require a change of hand position. An added advantage is that an improper elbow hook or loosely draped arm does not occur, as might happen with the elbow snap. Figure 5.7 illustrates a bad habit some wrestlers get into because they do not properly place strong forearm pressure on the bottom man's elbow.

Figure 5.6. Elbow grip.

Figure 5.7. Loose elbow pressure.

RIDING A FLAT MAN

Once a man is broken down to his stomach, he should be kept there as long as possible. The top wrestler needs to learn to control the man in the flat position on the mat. He does not want the man to get back up to his knees where an escape or reversal is possible. The top man works aggressively to control his opponent and secure a pinning combination. Before wrestlers learn how to turn a man over for a pin, they should learn top control. For a successful controlling ride, the top wrestler must use both arm control and hip and leg control.

Arm Control

Figure 5.8 shows a variety of techniques for controlling the bottom man's arms. Each of the arm holds can be used for keeping the defensive man under control and on his stomach. Techniques will be shown later to turn these controlling moves into pinning combinations. However, young or inexperienced wrestlers should learn the fundamentals of control before progressing to the more complicated techniques required to turn a man over for near fall points or a pin.

Success in each of these arm hold positions is somewhat related to the other positions. In fact, the major emphasis in this series of holds is on shifting from one position to another. The starting technique is not a critical element because the wrestler starts with whatever arm control he has after breaking the man down. However, an inside wrist hook on at least one arm is the basic fundamental of this series.

Figure 5.8. Riding flat man—arms.

Wrestler A has his left hand inside and grasps B's left wrist. A's right hand is over B's right shoulder and grasping B's right wrist. He rolls his knuckles forward as he tucks B's left arm under the chest and puts on a cross face with his right arm. He grips B's trapped left arm just above the elbow. From this position he can go to a cross face cradle (see step 8). A releases the cross face and snaps his right arm back to B's right upper arm and starts to sweep it to the rear. As he continues the pressure on B's right arm, he secures a bar arm. From this position A can go to a bar arm pin (see step 6). A releases B's right arm and allows him to straighten it out, then blocks B's right elbow with his hand. He releases the left wrist and puts on a cross face with his left arm as he slides off to the side to start a cross face cradle. If B extends his arms out in front and tries to raise his upper body, A pops forward with his hands to destroy the braces.

These techniques are practiced with the bottom man in a relatively passive position. He needs to react against pressure with only about half the normal resistance. The intent of the practice is to teach the top wrestler to recognize the possibilities for control and to shift from one arm-control hold to another. If the opponent straightens out his arm, the top man blocks the elbow and uses a cross face. If he lifts an elbow, the top man locks a bar arm. If he braces out, Wrestler A pops his hands out. If B tucks his hands back in, A grabs a wrist and rolls it under.

The top wrestler should always seek a position where at least one arm has inside control. At all times the controlling wrestler keeps chest and hip weight on the defensive wrestler.

Double Wrist Roll

The double wrist roll (Figure 5.9) illustrates the use of inside control on the bottom wrestler's wrists. Wrestler A rolls the knuckles of both hands forward and under while driving his forearms forward to post B's arm down under the chest. As A extends his left elbow forward and down against B's upper shoulder, and releases with his right hand, he maintains a lot of control but is off to the side where he can work for the pin.

Figure 5.9. Double wrist roll.

Hip and Leg Control

The second part of these controlling techniques for riding flat man involves the proper position of hips, legs, and chest. These are illustrated in Figure 5.10.

Wrestler A has a basic covering position. He squeezes his knees together to prevent B from getting them up for a brace to return to a hands-and-knees base position. A's hips are pressed firmly into B's buttocks, or Wrestler A can take a side covering position. His right knee is between B's legs, and his right heel is elevating B's left ankle to prevent B from getting to his knees. Again, hip pressure is essential.

Figure 5.10. Hips and legs control.

STEP 6

SIMPLE PINNING COMBINATIONS

A breakdown is an effective way of controlling a man to prevent an escape or a reverse, but it should more often be used as a method of turning the opponent over for a pin. Of all the techniques in wrestling, the ability to put a man on his back is the simplest for the benefit derived. Aggressively going for the pin will lead to decision victories even if a pin is not secured.

The secret of pinning success does not rest so much in holding a man down on the mat as it does in just keeping him turned over on his back. Many falls are lost because the top wrestler tried to keep a hold too long, when he should have just worked on controlling the man.

At the beginning level the half nelson pin and the bar arm pin will result in many victories. They are effective and easy to learn, both developing out of the riding flat man position. More experienced wrestlers will rely on the half nelson to catch opponents for quick near fall points. Many times the half nelson is available out of the double-leg tackle situation. From the double-leg pick-up (Figure 2.6), the offensive wrestler can put his opponent on the mat and drive in a half nelson for a pin. The bar arm is a good technique to use whenever the bottom man is stopped in a broken-down position on the mat.

HALF NELSON

The half nelson is a hold that can provide a simple pinning combination. Half nelson opportunities are present whenever the bottom man allows the top man to penetrate under the armpit and catch the head. The attacking wrestler should always be alert for opportunities to use a half nelson.

The half nelson is shown as a follow-up to a force nelson (Figure 6.1). (Other situations that lead to a half nelson will be discussed later in this book.)

Force Nelson

Wrestler A (on top) places his right forearm high on the back of B's head and grasps his right wrist with his left hand; his left arm is under B's upper left arm. For maximum pressure, A slides his right wrist over onto B's head. He extends his left forearm and elbow out and forward to gain maximum leverage. A continues the forcing action with both hands until he can extend his left arm in deep. He tries to get shoulder-to-shoulder with B. The driving motion is forward as well as up. A tucks B's head under as he keeps chest and shoulder pressure to turn B. He covers B's ear with his armpit as he turns B for a near fall. A slides his left knee up near B's head to increase the chest pressure.

Figure 6.1.   Half nelson from force nelson.

Position

The half nelson is an easy pin hold to use, but beginners often make a basic mistake that allows the bottom man to escape from the near fall position: The top man sometimes turns his body the wrong way (Figure 6.2). This incorrect position ends up with B's bridging up and over into a near fall position for B.

Figure 6.2.   Position—incorrect.

Figure 6.3 shows A in the correct position to prevent B from bridging and turning over. He has extended his right arm through the armpit area of B to trap the far arm of B. Additional leverage for a pin is gained by lifting B's head.

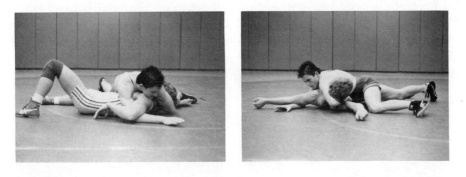

Figure 6.3.   Far arm block.

Counter by Bridging

If A does not block B's far arm, though, B bridges up to get room to move. B scoots his hips away and forces his arm across his chest. This action is quick and creates space for the arm. The bottom man can now turn his hips with a hip heist action and free himself from the half nelson (Figure 6.4).

Figure 6.4.   Counter to half nelson.

Head Lever

An effective breakdown that is easy to learn and that leads directly to the half nelson is the head lever (Figure 6.5). The head lever should be used as a combination breakdown and pin. The top man will find the technique simple to get on a beginning wrestler because the latter tends to keep his arms straight. The aggressive wrestler slips his head under his opponent's arm and goes for a half nelson pin.

The top wrestler drops his near hand to B's wrist. He rotates his hand to put pressure on B's wrist and keep the elbow straight. He puts the top of his head behind B's tricep. A pulls B's arm out to the side while driving B's shoulder to the mat. A steps his left foot out as a brace as he raises B's wrist. With a quick motion, A sinks his head under B's armpit while retaining his grip on the wrist. He drives his left hand deep as he secures a half nelson. He keeps his chest low and drives in as he moves forward to put B in a pin.

Figure 6.5. Head lever to half nelson.

Blocking Head Lever

The bottom wrestler can block the head lever and most other arm holds by keeping a good position with his hand, head, and elbows. The principle for protection also provides a good brace for movement: The bottom wrestler tries to keep the top of his hands where he can see them. By remembering this concept, he does not let his hands get trapped back under his chest. The basic position for protection uses the same motion as that shown for getting up from flat (Figures 1.20 and 1.21).

Figure 6.6 demonstrates the correct position, with the bottom wrestler's left hand out in front where he can see the top of it. His right hand is incorrectly placed back under his chest, where it can easily be caught by the top man.

Figure 6.6. Hand position.

BAR ARM

The bar arm (Figure 6.7) is a technique that provides the top wrestler a maximum amount of control while turning a defensive wrestler from his stomach to a pinning situation. The bar arm is executed slowly so that the defensive man cannot counter easily. The bar arm requires change of direction and position, but these movements are easily mastered even by beginning wrestlers. More advanced wrestlers will also find many opportunities to use the bar arm, a technique that also works against very good wrestlers.

The starting position for the bar arm is the riding flat man technique (Figure 5.8). The top man must have hip pressure and control before executing the bar arm.

Wrestler A (on top) has an underhook on B's right wrist and is posted over the top of B's left arm. He sweeps B's left arm back by hooking it above the elbow. A sits through with his right leg and keeps lots of pressure on B's lower back. A drives forward with his shoulders and body and rolls his right knuckles under to trap B's right arm under the body. A steps around towards B's head with his left leg. He drives forward and toward the head with his fist behind B's upper arm. A continues to drive B over, using pressure across and forward. He must keep B's elbow trapped in his armpit to avoid the twisting pressure of an illegal chicken wing. A forces B's shoulder down and behind the head to maintain maximum control. He applies this pressure by posting his left knee beyond B's head and by forcing forward and down with the back of his wrist in the armpit. The bar arm pin is completed by forcing B's shoulder to the mat. A must keep B's right arm trapped during this technique.

Position

Figure 6.8 emphasizes the need to elevate the bottom wrestler's near shoulder and to roll the far wrist under. These motions secure B's position on the mat by A's placing a great deal of weight on B's lower back. A does not pull B's arm back but drives the upper body over the top of the posted wrist.

Figure 6.9 shows the correct hand position with a clenched fist and forward driving action across the head. Proper execution of this position and of the elevate and tuck will result in many near fall points.

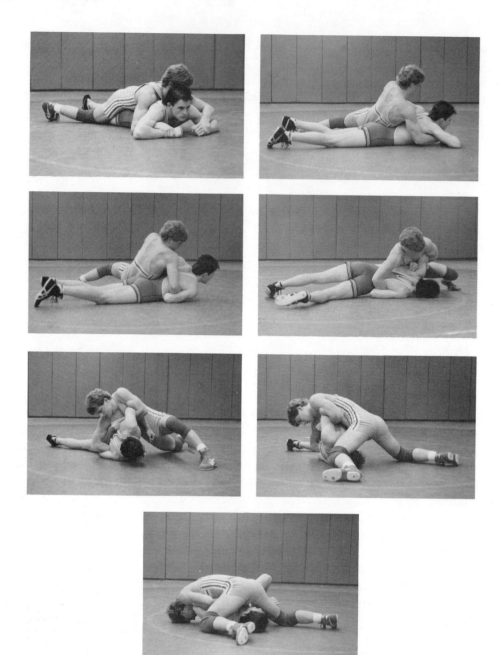

Figure 6.7. Bar arm.

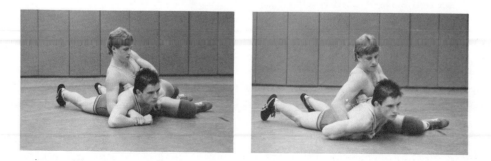

Figure 6.8. Elevate and tuck.

Figure 6.9. Hand position.

Pressure Points

Often the offensive wrestler can turn his opponent to his back for near fall points but is unable to secure a fall. Proper body position and execution can change near fall points to a pin. The key motion for the bar arm is to force the shoulder down and forward behind the head (Figure 6.9). This pressure posts the bottom man and allows the offensive wrestler two options with his right hand: He can hook elbows with B (Figure 6.10), or he can release the far arm and allow

Figure 6.10. Elbow hook.

B to turn (Figure 6.11). Proper execution of the elbow hook and the release of the far arm will turn those near falls into the ultimate success—a pin to end the match.

Throughout this book there are·many techniques where a clear distinction between correct and incorrect position may be difficult to see in the illustrations. The hand position and the proper forward posting of the shoulder in the bar arm are examples of this. Once a coach or wrestler feels the difference on the mat of the effectiveness of the proper pressure for the bar arm, however, he will recognize the proper position.

Figure 6.11.   Release far arm.

STEP 7

BEGINNING REVERSAL: SWITCH

Scoring two points for a reversal is one of the most difficult techniques to teach. It is often neglected as a skill even by the successful coach. You must teach reversal techniques, however, if your wrestlers are to become well-rounded.

A primary consideration for securing a reversal is to establish a sound base or platform from which to operate. The reversal is then executed rapidly and with power.

The most important criteria for a good base are a low center of gravity and braces spread wide. Both of these techniques require a great deal of practice time and effort. In addition, a fair degree of flexibility will lead to wide braces and a low center. These fundamentals were illustrated in step 1, ''Position and Movement.'' Failure to have a good base will lead to unsuccessful moves.

Wrestlers cannot execute reversal moves effectively unless they have a good down stance. Some of the movement drills were illustrated earlier. Returning to the base (Figure 1.18) and the knee scoot (Figure 1.17) are good examples. These techniques should be taught and practiced regularly.

The switch is a basic reversal that can be learned with diligent practice. The switch's fundamental hip-scissors motion is very similar to the hip heist, which was illustrated in Figure 1.22 and demonstrated in step 3 as part of the stand-up series. The switch is a highly effective move for both the beginner and the advanced wrestler. The coordination and agility to execute perfect switches may be lacking in young or inexperienced wrestlers. However, the change of direction, the heist motion, and the use of leverage and posts all build a foundation for later techniques. While the switch will help young wrestlers score quick points, it will also provide a sense of accomplishment.

A change of direction is part of the switch. Special care should be devoted to teaching the proper fundamentals of the switch because there are so many opportunities to use it as a reversal.

SWITCH AWAY

The fundamental reversal technique is the switch away. Often the switch away results in the bottom wrestler's change to a top position—a reversal. Sometimes the switch away is used as an escape. Regardless of the outcome—a reversal for two points or an escape for one—the basic movements of this technique stay basically the same. The hip movement, the coordinated change of upper body, the hip heist motion—all these skills will be developed (and also later adapted into several reversal or escape techniques). In a switch away, the emphasis is on movement out away from the top or controlling wrestler.

For Reversal

To secure a reversal, the bottom wrestler (A) has a wide base with his arms and knees (Figure 7.1). He drops his left elbow sharply to the inside, then shoots his left hand across in front of his right hand; at the same time, he pivots his right knee up to provide room for his left leg to sit through. A plants his left hand, sits through with his left leg, and catches his right elbow over B's right upper arm. A forces his right shoulder down, drops his head toward B's right hip, and scoots his hip away. A begins a hip heist action, which twists his hips away from A's grip; this action is accomplished by A's using the planted left foot and right shoulder as pivot points. A's right leg has snapped through to complete the hip twist. A reaches behind B's right knee to pull his body around for a reversal and to complete the move. He asserts control with a near-side cradle (detailed later).

For Escape

In the switch away for an escape technique, A extends his left arm a little farther forward and away while stepping out with his right foot. He attempts to get distance in the first movement. A sits through hard with his left leg and plants it forward and out. He has rotated his right hip and jammed his right elbow, right shoulder, and head down and into B's shoulder. A completes the movement with the hip heist action. As he extends and twists his hips, he comes free from B's grip and gains an escape (Figure 7.2).

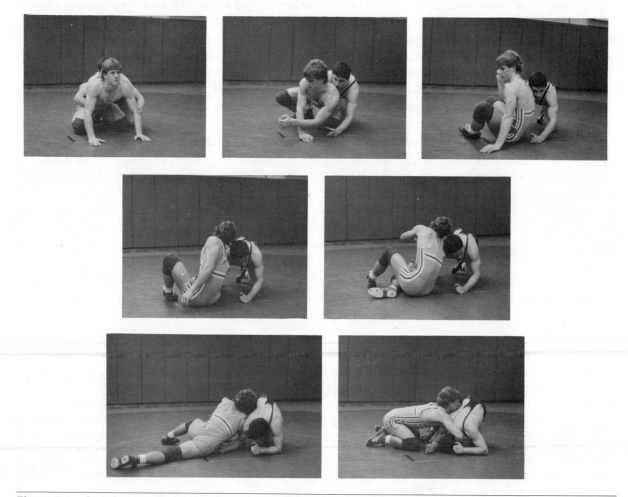

Figure 7.1. Switch away for reversal.

Figure 7.2. Switch away for escape.

The essential actions of the switch away involve two forceful twisting movements of the hips. The first action is a sit-through movement with the inside leg. This motion brings the inside leg from underneath the top wrestler. The bottom (left) leg then becomes the brace for the next hip movement. The right leg then thrusts back under the planted left foot. This leg heist action is rather like a scissors action. The first sit-through action brings the front of the hips up; the second heisting action turns them back down. Because several changes of direction are involved, the switch away must be practiced as a series of separate movements, then as a unified coordinated action.

Head and Elbow Positions

The head and elbow positions for the switch away are illustrated in Figure 7.3, with the bottom wrestler halfway through the move. He must twist his head and shoulders to "look" back toward B's hips.

The act of looking back into the hips forces the wrestler to twist his shoulders into such a position as to exert pressure down on the defensive man's arm and shoulder. More importantly, the position of the head cannot be achieved unless the hips are turned in the heisting motion.

Figure 7.3. Head and elbow positions.

Sometimes it is easier to teach young wrestlers to "look" than to get them to position their hips properly. This elbow-hook and head position is critical and must be diligently taught.

Often the bottom wrestler does not get his left elbow free from the top man's grip and then cannot complete his switch. Figures 7.4 and 7.5 show how to free the elbow at the start of and midway through the move, respectively. In each situation, the palm is turned up to rotate the elbow up and away.

Figure 7.4. Free elbow on start.

Figure 7.5. Free elbow midway.

Leg Grasp

Often the switch is made easier if the wrestler grasps his opponent's near leg to complete the move, as shown in Figure 7.6. Figure 7.7 shows the incorrect technique of reaching across the back instead of grasping the leg.

Figure 7.6. Grasp leg to complete move.

Figure 7.7. Incorrect grasp over body.

Scoot and Change Hips

Sometimes the wrestler does not get a successful sit-out motion with his hips. The Scoot and Change Hips Drill (Figure 7.8) will help wrestlers practice the correct technique.

Figure 7.8. Scoot and change hips drill.

Each of the movements illustrated in Figures 7.4 through 7.8 is only a part of the total technique for the switch away reversal or escape. Each separate part is an important element necessary for success in the move. Each should be practiced many times as a drill. For example, the free elbow on start (Figure 7.4) could be done 5 to 10 times on command in about 1 minute of practice time. Mastering this move is important because if the wrestler can't get his arms free, he can't complete the reversal. The Scoot and Change Hips Drill can be quickly done if partners cooperate. Often wrestlers lack the patience to drill, so you must organize practice sessions and insist on drilling as part of every practice.

SWITCH CLOSE

Sometimes the switch is effectively done by crowding back in (Figure 7.9) instead of moving out away from the top wrestler. The essential techniques are the same, but the wrestler just stays close with his hips and makes a shorter pivot. The crowding action is often helpful in freeing the inside elbow because the top man uses his left hand to catch his balance as he is pushed back to the side.

Figure 7.9.   Crowd to switch.

SWITCH DRILLS

The Power Switch Drill and the Scoot and Heist Drill (Figures 7.10 and 7.11, respectively) will really help wrestlers develop the switch.

These drills can be done quickly every day as part of the warm-up. Sometimes they can be put together with other moves in a series as change of direction is emphasized.

Having wrestlers execute a power switch, then a hip heist (Figure 1.22), then a duck-out (Figure 12.1) creates a feeling of continuous motion. These drills are also good conditioning activities if they are done hard and fast for 1 to 2 minutes with no hesitation. Additionally, you can observe and correct position and movement while your wrestlers drill with these.

Power Switch Drill

The Power Switch Drill (Figure 7.10) helps wrestlers learn the double hip change of direction used in all switches. This solo drill also helps wrestlers get the elbow hook and head position correct. You should have wrestlers lift the elbow high and drive it down hard as they change hips.

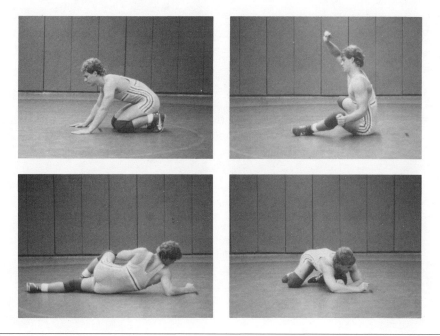

Figure 7.10. Power switch drill.

Scoot and Heist Drill

This second drill (Figure 7.11) helps wrestlers practice scooting the hips correctly and frees the inside arm. The Scoot and Heist Drill is started with the bottom man partway through his move but with his weight incorrectly placed on his left hip. He scoots his arm away as he rotates his hips.

Figure 7.11. Scoot and heist drill.

STEP 8

PINNING
FROM A CONTROL RIDE

This step teaches two pinning combinations—the cross face cradle and the double-arm lock. These moves have advantages for younger, more inexperienced wrestlers. The techniques begin from the riding flat man positions shown earlier. The bottom man is kept in control during the entire move. An additional advantage of teaching these techniques early is that each part of these moves is done slowly and deliberately; the young wrestler does not have to catch his opponent off guard and move fast.

The cross face cradle and double-arm lock pinning holds are quite simple, but they are very effective moves. A wrestler who can break his opponent down to the mat should immediately work for a pin. From the controlling position riding flat man, the wrestler now has two more pins to accompany the half nelson and bar arm (discussed in step 6).

CROSS FACE CRADLE

From the controlling ride shown in Figure 5.8, the best pinning combination is the cross face cradle (Figure 8.1). This is an easy move, and yet it is one that works even against quite skilled opponents. The cross face cradle does require change of direction, and it prepares young wrestlers for more complicated techniques that come later. The cross face cradle reinforces the idea of posting braces to assist in completing moves. It also builds on the in-the-lap position, which was introduced in Figure 1.25 and used in Figure 4.2, and the near-arm crotch-pry (Figure 5.3). The exact positions are not used, but the concept of keeping hips snug is part of each move.

A is controlling inside one wrist while blocking B's right elbow with his right hand. He applies the cross face on the ear and jaw and grasps above B's elbow. A keeps a great deal of chest pressure on B while lifting his left elbow to begin the turning pressure. A steps toward B's head and forces B's head and upper body away. He has planted his right hand inside B's right thigh so that B cannot move his hips or leg. A locks his hands around B's head, arm, and leg (this position is easier to see in Figure 8.2). A switches his hips vigorously. He pops his left thigh into and under B's hips to provide momentum to pull B back into his lap. A tips B's shoulders toward the mat for near fall points.

Figure 8.2 shows the same move from the other side, better illustrating the use of the hands.

Restricting Movement

The cross face cradle permits a certain amount of freedom of movement for the bottom man once he is on his back. Two techniques can be used by the top man to restrict this movement. One method of control is to press the forehead into B's temple while planting the bottom knee

Figure 8.1.   Cross face cradle.

into B's hip (Figure 8.3). The second method is to catch B's free leg with the heel of A's top leg and pull it down and in (Figure 8.4).

Turning Pressure

Most of the pressure required to turn B in the early stages of the cross face cradle is gained by proper elbow lifting and by stepping to the head so that the leg assists in the pushing action (Figure 8.5). During the initial turning action, the offensive wrestler must keep his chest hard against the down wrestler's upper back. If the top wrestler releases chest pressure, the bottom man can lift his hips and escape the hold.

The offensive wrestler should not try to hurry this technique. He scoots B's head and shoulders a little at a time and forces them down to the leg that is blocked. Then he locks his hands. The tipping action is then done quickly, turning the defensive wrestler over onto his back.

Figure 8.2. Far side.

Figure 8.3. Head and knee control.

Figure 8.4. Leg control.

Figure 8.5. Turning pressure.

DOUBLE-ARM LOCK

Sometimes the defensive wrestler turns his bottom arm and chest toward the top man as the cross face cradle is being applied. This defensive action neutralizes the elbow pressure and does prevent the technique shown in the cross face cradle. However, the offensive wrestler can turn this counter to his advantage. He merely pulls the bottom arm under and changes to a double-arm lock (Figure 8.6). This action results in near fall points or a possible pin.

The bottom wrestler (B) has countered A's cross face cradle by turning toward A. Thus, A shifts his right hand from the leg plant position and grasps B's bottom arm with both hands. He keeps his chest tight, controlling the other arm as well. Exerting a lifting, twisting action on both arms, A steps toward B's head and into a near fall position.

Figure 8.6. Double arm lock.

INTERMEDIATE WRESTLING SKILLS

The techniques illustrated in this second stage of steps of *Successful Wrestling* are designed for a 2nd-year wrestler. These steps require changes of direction, more coordination, and more complex sequences of action. All of the skills in this stage build on the techniques learned in steps 1 through 8.

You should have your wrestlers review and drill on the techniques learned in Stage 1, ''Beginning Wrestling Skills.'' As wrestlers demonstrate proficiency in those moves, you should introduce the first steps of this second stage.

This stage begins with Step 9, a set of takedown moves. You should then teach the double wrist ride (Step 10) for control and for pinning. Step 11 shows the standing switch as a reversal from a variety of positions. Mat escapes or reversals are illustrated in step 12. A series of rides and pins are shown in step 13. Stage 2 concludes with several takedown counters.

Stage 2 is organized in a set of progressively more difficult steps with one exception: The takedown counters in step 14 could be introduced earlier.

You may be tempted to rush into all six of the steps at once, but you should carefully program the progressive introduction and practice of the moves demonstrated in these steps. It is more important for wrestlers to become highly skilled in a more limited set of techniques than for them to attempt skills beyond their maturity or coordination levels.

Wrestlers who have progressed through Stage 2 of *Successful Wrestling* will have acquired mastery of three or four takedowns, two or three escapes or reversals, and a limited set of rides and pins. These wrestlers will have climbed the winner's stand several times, winning 70 to 80 percent of their matches against good opponents.

INTERMEDIATE TAKEDOWNS

Although the principal objective of wrestling is to gain a pin, most matches are decided on points, particularly when wrestlers are skilled. Getting a takedown is the most important method of gaining enough points to win a match by decision.

To be successful in scoring takedowns, a wrestler must have confidence in his ability to take his opponent to the mat. It is not enough for the wrestler merely to think he can take his opponent down—he must know he can.

Body position and footwork are important to provide a proper base for movement; the staggered stance gives this base. The wrestler uses the inside tie-up shown in Figure 1.10. All takedowns illustrated in this book start from the same basic tie and stance. The two takedowns demonstrated in this step are similar in their beginning moves, although the finishing moves are different. A wrestler who becomes skilled in the technique of one will find success with the other.

The variations and follow-up techniques of the single-leg attack are advanced skills, though. You may decide to hold some of the lifting and tripping techniques until a later stage of your wrestlers' development. Against really good wrestlers, the single-leg attack is a very important skill. Some world and Olympic champions rely on the single-leg as their key to successful wrestling and gold medals. Often young or inexperienced wrestlers lack the coordination and speed necessary for success in the snatching technique. Therefore, most of the emphasis at this point is on the simpler motions. The techniques shown can be accomplished successfully by average wrestlers. Of course, considerable drill work is needed on all phases of the single-leg attack. You can drill team members on any aspect of the techniques with passive or active resistance by the defensive man.

OUTSIDE FIREMAN'S CARRY

A simple yet effective takedown that should be mastered early by your wrestlers in their quest for success is the outside fireman's carry (Figure 9.1). This technique is effective by itself, but it also acts as an important setup for the single-leg attack.

The outside fireman's carry is particularly effective against tired or inexperienced wrestlers. Late in a match, tired wrestlers tend to lean or push in. They are easily dumped forward with the outside fireman's carry. Inexperienced wrestlers also have a tendency to lean or push; therefore, the move works well.

More experienced wrestlers will probably keep a better stance. They may not be as susceptible to the outside fireman's carry. However, the first three motions of the carry lead directly into the single-leg attack.

The starting position for the outside fireman's carry is the same as that for all takedown moves: The inside tie on the opponent's elbow gives control of the arm, the staggered stance gives a position for maximum penetration, and the elbow hook assures that the offensive wrestler gains control of his opponent's leg.

Wrestler A, on the left, has an inside elbow tie with his left arm and a collar block with his right. He pushes with his right forearm enough to get B to react back into him. A shoots his right knee just outside B's left toe while pulling forward and down with his left hand. This pulling action shifts B's weight to the right foot. A continues to swing his body weight back toward his right foot as he pulls hard on B's right arm. By lifting up and around on B's left leg and pulling hard on B's right arm, A dumps B onto his right shoulder. A completes the move by going into a front pancake position for a pin or near fall points. Sometimes he may only be able to go behind B for takedown points.

Figure 9.1.   Outside fireman's carry.

Hand Cut and Elbow Hook

The attacking wrestler must cut his hand quickly down his opponent's side (Figure 9.2) and catch his elbow behind the knee (Figure 9.3).

Figure 9.2. Hand cut.

Figure 9.3. Elbow hook.

The attacking wrestler must go directly at the left foot and leg of his opponent. He steps directly at, and drops his knee just outside, the defensive man's foot. He cuts his hand straight down the body in the closest line possible. You must emphasize these direct penetrating actions to keep wrestlers from making wide, sweeping reaches that will not be successful. If a wrestler puts his knee to the mat very far outside the opponent's foot, he would actually be moving away from his target. If he sweeps the right hand around instead of cutting it straight down, the opponent can block the arm or would have time to move his leg.

Set Up

A good inside elbow tie and quick forward pull are important to set up a successful outside fireman's carry. The pulling motion forces the defensive wrestler to shift his weight to the right leg (Figure 9.4). When he steps or shifts weight to his right, he will not be able to move his left leg, which is being attacked.

Plant and Spin Drill

The outside fireman's carry uses a lot of rotating and twisting force. The head is kept tucked in close, but the arms and shoulders rotate. The right knee is planted and then rotated around with the hips. This technique is somewhat complicated because of the rotation and change of direction. Still, most average wrestlers should be able to master this very effective takedown. Coordination and change of direction are taught while drilling on this technique. Figure 9.5 shows the Plant and Spin Drill, which helps teach change of direction.

Figure 9.4. Pull to set up.

Figure 9.5. Plant and spin drill.

SINGLE-LEG ATTACK

One of the fundamental takedowns is the single-leg attack. This technique has several variations, but all emphasize the concentrated attack on one leg. Though this attack concentrates on one leg, it uses a more complicated change in hand and body position than the outside fireman's carry, but develops naturally from it. Although it is an excellent leg attack even against quite skilled opponents, it has a set of simple movements and body position fundamentals.

The single-leg attack is an aggressive penetrating movement designed to control one of the defensive wrestler's legs. It can be initiated from an open tie position without touching the defensive wrestler, or it can be initiated out of the inside tie-up (Figure 1.10). Penetration must be swift and straight in. The single-leg attack can be done by going to the knees or by staying on the feet and stepping in.

Single-Leg Attack From Outside Fireman's Carry

Wrestler A (back to camera) has started the outside fireman's carry but does not get B's right shoulder pulled down as far as necessary to successfully complete the move (Figure 9.6). His elbow is firmly hooked at B's knee, and his right knee is planted close to B's foot. He releases B's right arm and grasps B's left leg with both arms in deep; the last photo shows the tight grasp on B's left leg. A keeps his head in deep to the hip area and clamps B's thigh to his chest.

The single-leg can also be attacked directly from the open stance as shown in Figure 9.7. You should have your wrestlers practice penetrating to the single-leg attack. All your wrestlers can

Figure 9.6. Single from outside fireman's carry.

Figure 9.7. Single-leg attack from open stance.

be paired off. On command, one wrestler of each pair shoots the single from the open stance at least 10 times. Partners can switch roles after each penetration or after sets of 5 or 10.

Head Position

One error that wrestlers commonly make while learning the single-leg attack is incorrect positioning of the head (Figure 9.8a). You must monitor all drills and practice sessions to be sure wrestlers tuck their heads on the inside, as shown in Figure 9.8b.

Because B's most common counter to the single-leg attack is a whizzer—in this case with his left arm—and pressure on A's head, A has practically eliminated that counter with his head position. However, the position with head outside the hips is not necessarily a bad position. Later illustrations of the high-crotch series will show positions very similar to this one. Nevertheless, in the single-leg attack, the head needs to be tucked inside the opponent's hips.

The techniques shown in Figures 9.6 through 9.8 illustrate the single-leg attack position as one down on the mat, the attacking wrestler going to one or both knees and pivoting behind the opponent's leg. He should then stand and lift B's leg from the mat, as shown in Figure 9.7.

a   b

Figure 9.8. Head position—incorrect/correct.

Leg and Arm Trips

Once he has the leg up, Wrestler A may use any of several methods to put his opponent on the mat and secure takedown points. Two of these methods are shown in the next two photo series. Both are tripping motions: Figure 9.9 shows a leg trip, and Figure 9.10 shows an arm trip.

Follow-Up Moves

Sometimes the defensive wrestler is able to sprawl and partially block the single-leg attack. The offensive wrestler then needs some follow-up techniques to get the sprawling wrestler into a position where his leg can be picked up.

Figure 9.9. Leg trip.

Figure 9.10. Arm trip.

Climb Stairs

B, with his back to camera, has sprawled his legs back and lowered his hips (Figure 9.11). A cannot get to B's knee for control, so he slides his right wrist up to B's hip joint and locks his hands at the base of the singlet. A's left hand must be palm-up in the grip. A climbs up into B. The action is like climbing stairs on hands and knees. He keeps his hips down, raises his shoulders and head, and climbs up into B. Because B will usually keep his feet planted, A is able to rotate him up to a standing position. A then steps to his right and starts to lift. A drops his grip to B's knee and completes the move.

Sometimes the attacking wrestler needs to post his hand on the mat either to help him lift (Figure 9.12) or to spin around his opponent's leg (Figure 9.13).

Back Step

Another effective technique for completing the single-leg attack is to pick up the opponent's leg, then use a back step to drop B to the mat (Figure 9.14). This technique uses a pulling motion

Figure 9.11. Climb stairs.

Figure 9.12.   Post and lift drill.

Figure 9.13.   Pivot and elbow down drill.

away from the defensive man. This motion keeps the man off balance and drops him in a direction where he has no braces.

The preferred technique for the single-leg attack by experienced wrestlers is to penetrate from the open, pick up the knee, and use either the back step (Figure 9.14) or the leg trip (Figure 9.9). A highly skilled wrestler usually does not touch his knee to the mat. He uses a level change,

Figure 9.14. Back step.

quick penetration with his hands, and more of a snatching action with his hands. This technique requires explosive forward motion, followed by a quick movement to the rear.

Jam and Jerk

Successful completion of the single-leg attack is dependent upon getting the defensive man to the mat after picking up his leg. Often the defensive man counters by hopping around the mat on one foot and is able to fight free of the controlling grasp of the offensive wrestler. The jam and jerk technique (Figure 9.15) moves the control from the thigh to the ankle or knee. This position gives the attacking man the advantage.

A has a good clamp on B's thigh, but B has been successful in keeping his balance on one foot. A steps forward with his outside foot and jams his head and shoulder into B, causing B's weight to shift backward. As A steps back quickly and jerks on B's leg, he slides his hands to the lower leg and ankle. A now underhooks B's ankle with both forearms and elevates B's leg with an explosive lift, which brings B's other leg off the mat. Without a brace, B drops to his hips on the mat, with A covering.

Figure 9.15. Jam and jerk.

STEP 10

CONTROLLING RIDES TO PINS

The top wrestler has two primary tasks: He needs to prevent the bottom man from scoring points with escapes and reversals, and he needs to put the man on his back for near fall points or a pin. These two tasks are compatible; the best controlling rides are ones that threaten the defensive wrestler with being put on his back.

DOUBLE WRIST RIDE

Many times in a match, the top wrestler wants to control his opponent in order to protect a lead. He should also be working for a pin but doesn't want to give up escape or reversal points. The double wrist ride, with two-on-one control, provides maximum control of the bottom wrestler. It can be secured out of several positions such as stand-ups, near-arm breakdowns, or whenever the top wrestler can encircle his opponent's waist or chest and secure a wrist ride.

A, on top, has a tight grip on B's right arm with both hands (Figure 10.1). The left hand is on the wrist, and the right is on the forearm. His hips are down and covering B. A tucks B's arm under the chest through a combination of rolling his knuckles forward to the mat while driving forward with his forearms in B's armpits. A keeps his weight on B's hips and forces his right elbow forward so that a great deal of pressure is exerted downward by his forearm on B's upper arm. A shifts his body slightly to the side to increase the pressure on B's arm.

A has completed the double wrist to a position of control (Figure 10.2). He then hops across B's body to the opposite side, where he maintains wrist control with his left hand. A's right hand goes from the controlling pressure on the arm to a position near B's hips. A pulls vigorously on B's wrist and drives with his chest. His right hand is lifting on B's left inside thigh. He can shift to a half nelson with the left hand or go to a turk ride, whose description follows.

Figure 10.1. Double wrist ride.

Figure 10.2.   Double wrist to half nelson.

INSIDE TURK

The inside turk (Figure 10.3) is a leg lift technique that is an excellent way to score near fall points. The move is a good follow-up to the double wrist. The move is aggressive, yet it retains the advantage or control position. This position also is one that can follow out of many other combinations. Once wrestlers recognize this "leg-in" position, they will discover many opportunities to use it.

Figure 10.3.   Inside turk.

Wrestler A has a double wrist ride and is off to the side. He has pulled B's arm under and shifted his weight forward. A reaches back between B's legs and grasps the right leg just above the knee. He keeps chest pressure on B while lifting B's right leg by driving in and forward. He steps over B's left leg above the knee while continuing to lift the right leg. A uses a back arch motion to twist B's hips. By lifting with the leg and pulling on the arm, he turns B's shoulders to the mat for near fall points.

All of these last three techniques are very effective pinning holds that maintain control of the bottom man in the process. However, each has a special feel. You need to go through them slowly and concentrate on position and pressure points. Often you will need to physically place both wrestlers in the correct positions and point out the proper location and direction of pressure.

DOUBLE BAR ARM

The double bar arm (Figure 10.4) is not a particularly difficult pinning combination and probably could be taught earlier in the program. The double bar arm starts from the same position of control on the mat as the bar arm (step 6) but provides more turning power.

It is a special-situation technique, one not often used. An offensive wrestler might employ the double bar arm against a man who goes into a sit-out (step 12) and then does not move. Another use comes when the attacker has turned the bottom man but has not been able to get

Figure 10.4. Double bar arm.

a pin because of the defensive wrestler's good, high bridge. Because the double bar arm gives almost complete control of both arms, it prevents the opponent from bridging.

Obviously, the top man must catch the bottom man out of position or be much stronger to get the double bar arm from either the sit-out or the flat position. Usually this technique is used by a superior wrestler against one not so skilled, and whenever any opponent gives him the opportunity.

The top wrestler has a near-side bar arm, controlling B flat on the mat (Figure 10.4). He then overhooks B's far arm, pulls it back, and hooks both arms in a double bar position. A steps to B's head and turns B's shoulders to the mat by stepping his hips across B's head and shoulders. A completes the double bar arm by sitting through with his right leg. By keeping both arms hooked and forcing up into B's back, A should get a pin.

Counter Sit-Out

The double bar arm sometimes can be put on as a counter on a man who uses a sit-out (see Figure 12.8). Often the opponent will plant his hands beside his hips as he scoots to maintain his balance. The top wrestler can then drive into him hard and secure the double bar arm (Figure 10.5). This hold becomes a controlling ride that can be turned into near fall points or a pin only by dumping the defensive wrestler to his side and stomach, where he can then be turned as shown in Figure 10.4.

Figure 10.5. Counter sit-out.

TURK RIDE

The turk ride (Figure 10.6) is really a very aggressive leg ride designed to control the bottom man. It is very effective as a move to secure back points and even as a pinning hold. The turk ride is taught from a position on top of a defensive wrestler who is on his stomach on the mat, similar to riding flat man (step 5); the proper hip position can be most easily discovered from

Figure 10.6. Turk ride.

this position. Later the turk ride can be learned from a position on the hands and knees; this more advanced technique is shown in step 16 with other leg rides.

The top wrestler is controlling the defensive wrestler on the mat. He keeps his hips down while hooking his right heel under B's left ankle from the inside. A raises his right heel to lift B's ankle and grasps B's left ankle with his right hand. By pulling up and forward, he gains clearance to put his left foot under B's thigh. A hangs onto the ankle as he shifts his weight to his right hip. A scoops his left foot under B's leg above the knee and catches his left toe over his right knee for a figure four. He thrusts his upper body forward and his hips down while lifting hard with his right heel. This action turns B's hips. A continues to exert downward pressure with his legs. He catches B across the chin or forehead to keep him stretched out. He controls

B's head while looking away and pulling, scoring near fall points. A may catch B's left arm high in the armpit in a whizzer position as an alternative way of controlling the upper body for a near fall or pin.

Catch with Straight Leg

Sometimes the defensive wrestler will not allow his leg to flex at the knee as the top man lifts at the ankle. In this way, he prevents the top wrestler from catching his ankle as A did in Figure 10.6. The technique illustrated in Figure 10.7 shows A how to put on the turk ride when the bottom man keeps his leg straight. If B leaves his leg straight, A can lift at the ankle enough to get his left heel under the knee.

Figure 10.7.   Catch with straight leg.

Leg Action and Chest Position

The leg action required for the turk ride should be practiced as a warm-up exercise. The back arch (Figure 10.8) stretches the legs, back, and shoulders while preparing the wrestlers for the lifting, twisting motion necessary to be successful in the turk ride series. The groin stretch (Figure 1.14) is an exercise that helps prepare wrestlers to keep their hips flat and their knees out wide. This latter position is necessary for scooping the feet under and rotating the knees out as required in the turk ride for maximum pressure on the opponent's hips.

In the turk ride, proper chest position for control of the head is necessary. The offensive wrestler does not want to turn his shoulders down under the bottom wrestler (Figure 10.9a). Instead, he keeps his head high, his chest facing the mat, and his right arm posted as a brace (Figures 10.9b and c).

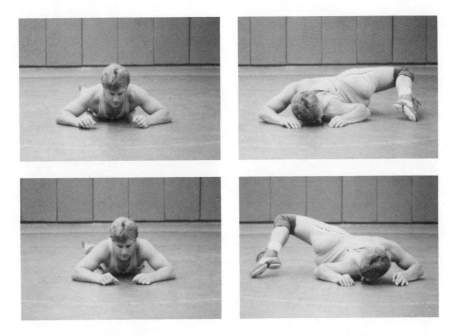

Figure 10.8. Back arch.

Figure 10.9. Shoulder position—incorrect/correct.

STEP 11

REVERSALS
FROM STANDING POSITION

The standing switch is an excellent move to teach intermediate wrestlers. It can be used by the bottom man when the top man has a waist lock in the standing position. Sometimes the bottom wrestler cannot prevent the riding man from clasping his hands around the body. He may try the cage fight moves learned in Figure 3.3, but may lose that battle.

The bottom wrestler can use the standing switch in three basic ways: (a) He may use a lot of hip action and turn back in from his feet; (b) he can fall forward and hit the switch as he lands; or (c) he can start the standing switch on the way down when his opponent tries to return him to the mat with a back heel block.

Often the bottom wrestler can get to his feet but is unable to break the top man's grip. Or, if the bottom man has a good standing switch, he may get to his feet in a stand-up without worrying too much about preventing his opponent from locking his hands in a rear standing position.

The standing switch (Figure 11.1) is a move that requires good hip motion and the correct pivot action. Generally, a wrestler who has a good switch on the mat (step 7) can execute an effective standing switch.

The key to success in the standing switch technique is aggressive hip motion. The bottom wrestler must throw his hips hard back and forth as he sets up the standing switch from the erect position. When he does start the move, he must drop his hip and pivot hard with his shoulders. On the standing switch from the falling forward position, the wrestler must lunge forward and then pivot back in hard. When he is put down to the mat by his opponent, he posts hard and starts an aggressive counter.

The bottom wrestler (A) has come to his feet but is being controlled by the top wrestler. He starts the standing switch by dropping his hips as he steps forward with his left foot. A pivots on his right foot and drops his hips down in a clockwise motion. He forces his right arm and shoulder down as he starts the arm action necessary to grasp B's right knee. He must drop hard and pivot at the same time, forcing his head and shoulder into B's thigh. This pressure breaks B's grip. A locks his hands around B's thigh as he steps around quickly with his left foot in the pivot. A continues to pivot and comes to a rear standing position for reversal points.

HIP MOTION DRILL

The bottom wrestler must use a lot of hip motion to get freedom enough to drop down to the standing switch. He does this by whipping his hips to his right, then left. This action is shown in Figure 11.2.

Figure 11.1. Standing switch.

Figure 11.2. Hip motion drill.

FALLING FORWARD SWITCH

Sometimes the bottom wrestler can simply lunge forward to his hands and knees (Figure 11.3). As he hits the mat, the top man must release his waist lock. The bottom man then executes a good switch for reversal points.

Figure 11.3.   Falling forward switch.

COUNTER HEEL BLOCK

The top wrestler may pull his opponent backward with a heel block (Figure 4.4). The bottom wrestler first allows his body to float with the action, but then he starts a hard hip rotation and plants his feet, hips, and hands so that he can execute the switch as soon as he hits the mat (Figure 11.4).

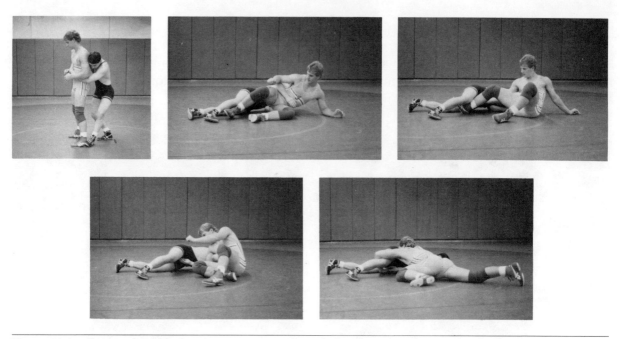

Figure 11.4. Counter heel block.

COUNTER FORWARD TRIP

Anytime a wrestler is taken to the mat, he should try to land with braces and begin an escaping or reversing move. In step 4 the forward trip and lift were used to return a standing wrestler to the mat. To counter, often the bottom wrestler can hit a switching motion just as he makes contact with the mat (Figure 11.5). Once a wrestler has learned the standing switch, he will find many opportunities to use it.

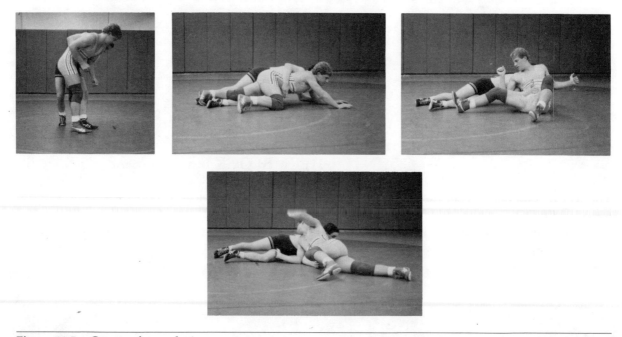

Figure 11.5. Counter forward trip.

STEP 12

MAT ESCAPES

One of the very early techniques learned by wrestlers was the stand-up for escapes (step 3). The stand-ups were introduced among the first techniques because beginning wrestlers need to learn to gain the mobility that is possible in the standing position.

The stand-ups did not require extensive change of direction and did not demand coordination. These aspects are required in this step's series of mat escapes, however. Included here are three techniques—the duck-out, the sit-out, and the Granby tuck roll. Each requires movement, change of direction, and proper body position.

Each escape in this step starts with a similar motion and is executed in close to the top man. In contrast, in the switch away (Figure 7.2) and the stand-up (Figure 3.1),the bottom man tried to get distance and clear himself away from his opponent. The techniques shown in this step, though, are done by the bottom wrestler's having the top man stay in a covering position and in contact with the bottom man's back. Furthermore, much hip motion is required; a good tight shoulder tuck is also part of each move.

Each of the mat escapes in this step complements the others. Together they give the developing wrestler a very effective set of combinations. Any one of the moves could be changed into the others; therefore, the duck-out, the Granby tuck roll, and the short sit-out series can be used one after the other in a variety of combinations. Because they are so similar in their initial motions, the top man may not recognize which one is being used.

DUCK-OUT

Every good wrestler should learn to turn back into his opponent as a change of pace because so many moves of the bottom wrestler are out and away. The switch, the stand-up, and the hip heist all depend on breaking free from the top man's control of the near arm.

The duck-out (Figure 12.1) starts the motion away from the controlling top man, then comes back in tight to the inside. The duck-out is executed from a sit-through position similar to the start of a switch (Figure 7.1). The wrestler must then come back in hard and low; the key to success is a continuous pivot on the left shoulder and arm.

For the duck-out, the bottom wrestler (A) starts with his weight back over his hips. He sits through with his left leg in a motion that resembles the beginning of a hip heist or a switch. He stays close in, with his back to the top man. Wrestler A tucks his left elbow in and drives his shoulder and head to the mat. He continues the pivot on his shoulder and throws his right leg around low and hard. He must keep his shoulder posted on the mat and pivot around it. A twists his hips to a hips-up position on his knees and begins to pull his head and shoulders out. He thrusts his left arm up and back as his head pops out. This arm thrust is critical because it prevents B from following the spin. A finishes the move by going behind for the reversal. (In the photo sequence, the top wrestler has not followed the bottom man as he would in real

Figure 12.1. Duck-out.

competition. These pictures were posed to most clearly illustrate the technique of the wrestler executing the move.)

The correct position of the elbow and shoulder and the movement and position of the legs are very important, particularly when the top man follows closely. Figure 12.2 shows the incorrect position of the elbow, the shoulder, the head, and the bottom leg. The bottom wrestler has not fully committed himself to the move. His elbow is not tucked in far enough. He has straightened his inside leg, and his head is not on the mat. He will not be successful from this position. Teach your wrestlers the correct position as shown in Figure 12.1.

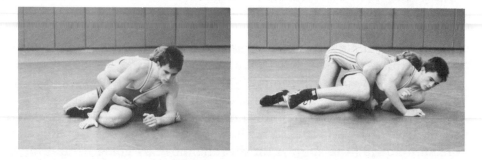

Figure 12.2. Incorrect position.

Duck-Out Solo Drill

The tuck and spin position required for a good duck-out should be practiced every day. It teaches coordination and movement. The Duck-Out Solo Drill (Figure 12.3) is a good team warm-up at the beginning of practice because it requires rapid movement. Also, use this drill for 15 to 30 seconds at intervals during practice as one of a series of cardiovascular drills. Furthermore, you could use it at a slower pace at the end of practice as a cool-down drill.

The Duck-Out Solo Drill should be done on the whistle as a drill. Wrestlers should first hit one side, then the other. The entire team can practice sitting out, spinning, and whipping the arm and head around in duck-out motions. You can observe them and easily detect wrestlers who are incorrectly executing the move. You should first emphasize correct position, then gradually increase the speed.

Figure 12.3. Duck-out solo drill.

Long-Sit Duck-Out

A variation of the duck-out that usually results in an escape is done with a movement out away from the top man. The basic movements of this long-sit duck-out are identical to the standard duck-out except for the first movement (Figure 12.4). The bottom wrestler executes a kick-through with the inside leg and tries to create distance from the man in control. After the shoulder spin, the bottom man will probably be out in front, and as he comes through with his left elbow, he will be facing his opponent for an escape.

The long-sit duck-out is similar in its first movement to the hip heist (Figure 1.22). The bottom wrestler pops his inside leg through as he tries to get distance away from the top man. However, instead of continuing the hip and posting action, the wrestler changes direction and comes back to the inside.

After wrestlers have learned both moves, have them drill on the techniques by issuing the command ''Hip heist'' or ''Long-sit,'' then blowing the whistle to start the action. You should have wrestlers alternate the motions: hip heist, long-sit, hip heist. Self-motivated wrestlers can practice these moves independently, first at a moderate speed, then at full speed.

The duck-out is an excellent move as a reversal technique. Additionally, the movement sets up the Granby tuck roll. The similarity of the initial positions and the spinning movement on the shoulder creates the proper Granby tuck roll position with the arm hook inside the leg (Figure 12.5).

Figure 12.4.   Long-sit to duck-out.

GRANBY TUCK ROLL

The easiest Granby roll to teach is the Granby tuck roll, a modification of the more advanced regular Granby roll. The Granby tuck roll is a good move to teach after wrestlers learn the duck-out.

Against a wrestler with good movement, the bottom wrestler often cannot complete the duck-out because the top man follows so closely that the bottom man cannot get his left elbow and shoulder clear. A Granby tuck roll (Figure 12.5) should then be used.

The bottom wrestler (A) starts the short-sit position as he would for a duck-out. He grasps B's wrist with his right hand. A drops to his shoulder and head with a quick elbow tuck. He starts his right leg stepping around low and hard to get spinning motion. A pivots up with his hips. He has his head and shoulder down and keeps a tight grip on B's right wrist. As B follows A's hips, A thrusts his left elbow and arm up through B's legs. A's left thumb is rotated down and up as he extends his arm. A overhooks B's thigh from the inside and tucks his right hip and leg under. His left leg begins a driving motion toward B's head. A pulls B's right shoulder down by rotating his hips through in a scissors action, almost a reverse hip heist, as he elevates B's hips with his left arm through the legs. A completes the move and scores both·a reversal and a near fall. A keeps B on his back by maintaining the lock on B's wrist and leg.

Figure 12.5.   Granby tuck roll.

Spinning Motion

Two very important parts of the Granby tuck roll are a spinning motion on the shoulder and a swinging motion with the left arm to continue momentum. These techniques require motion and position rather than strength. Figure 12.6 emphasizes how to maintain the spinning motion on the shoulder to set up the Granby tuck roll. The proper motion and position of the left arm are also shown.

The Granby tuck roll is highly effective if a wrestler is willing to practice it and develop the spinning, lifting motion necessary. The duck-out and the Granby tuck roll make a very effective combination. If the top man doesn't follow the spin, the bottom man completes the duck-out. If the top man does attempt to follow the spin, the wrestler throws his left arm up through the crotch and completes the Granby tuck roll.

SIT-OUT SERIES

The sit-out series provides a position from which a number of techniques can be executed. The basic position of the sit-out (Figure 12.7) is with the wrestler's weight on his buttocks, his feet out in front with his knees lifted from the mat and his elbows tucked into his middle. The sit-out

Figure 12.6. Shoulder spin.

Figure 12.7. Sit-out position.

should be started with the sit-through motion used for the duck-out. The wrestler must protect himself from being snapped back to his shoulders or from being controlled by the top wrestler.

The basic position presents the base from which to execute one of a series of techniques, depending upon the actions of the top wrestler. If the top man hangs his head or one arm over the shoulder, the bottom man grabs it and pivots away in a motion similar to the duck-out (Figure 12.1). If the top man keeps his hands around the waist area, the bottom man uses a switch for the reversal.

The bottom man (A) goes from his basic stance in the bottom position to a sit-through with his inside leg. He leans back into B just a little bit. A completes his move to a sit-out by bringing his outside foot forward. He is in a balanced position, with his heels planted as braces and with his arms in tight to prevent B from hooking them.

The top man may counter the sit-out by attempting to snap the man back. The bottom man corrects his balance by scooting back into the top man (Figure 12.8).

Figure 12.8. Scoot for balance.

Options

Once the bottom wrestler has learned to move quickly to the sit-out position and can maintain a good base from there, he has several options as escape or reversal moves. These are illustrated in the next four figures. He may drop to his shoulder for a spin to a duck-out (Figure 12.9) or scoot away and hit a power switch (Figure 12.10).

The head spin (Figure 12.11) and the arm spin (Figure 12.12) are very similar in technique. The bottom wrestler grasps whatever hangs over his shoulder—the head or the arm. He throws his arm up toward his head to catch the head or arm and drops his shoulder on the other side. He must pivot hard and rotate his hips to come up. He must not scoot his hips away during either move or he will get trapped on his back. He should be alert to react the instant B hangs his head or arm over either side.

You can use these techniques as a solo drill. Give the command ''Sit-out''; then command ''Left'' or ''Right'' to suggest the imaginary top man's overhooking on the left or right side. The wrestlers then complete the spin and return to their hands and knees in preparation for the next command. Drilling 2 or 3 minutes each day will help your wrestlers develop spontaneous responses for these two spins. This drill can also be practiced with partners who deliberately hang either head or arm over one shoulder or the other.

All of the sit-out series techniques need to be practiced so that reaction to the top man's action becomes more automatic. This series is worked from the mat and requires a short-coupled spinning action similar to that of the duck-out (Figure 12.1). Although speed is important here,

Figure 12.9. Spin to duck-out.

Figure 12.10. Scoot to power switch.

Figure 12.11. Head spin.

Figure 12.12. Arm spin.

explosive power is not. The series is of medium difficulty. Coordination and change of direction are required, but the individual moves are simple and can be taught one at a time.

Countering the Sit-Out

The most effective counter for the top man to use against the sit-out series is the chest pressure counter (Figure 12.13). The wrestler in the riding position follows the sit-through motion of the down wrestler. He keeps his chest in tight and in fact drives hard into the wrestler's back. This action posts weight in such a way that movement by the bottom man is difficult. The top man should not reach over with his arms or head. He tries to tip the bottom man to one side or the other and follow him.

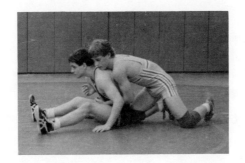

Figure 12.13. Chest pressure counter.

STEP 13

INTERMEDIATE RIDES AND PINS

The blanket ride and the near-side cradle are effective techniques that preserve control for the top man while affording many near fall points. Each technique involves wrapping the defensive man's upper body and legs into a tightly rolled ball. The top man literally cradles the bottom man to his chest while riding or turning him.

BLANKET RIDE

The blanket ride is discussed first because it is a controlling ride and breakdown that leads directly to the near-side cradle. The top man must use agility and motion to maintain control. The action must be aggressive and the pressure continuous. The term *blanket ride* comes from the concept of covering the opponent. Parts of the top wrestler's body are positioned on all sides of the bottom wrestler (Figure 13.1).

Figure 13.1. Blanket ride—covering.

The top man (A) uses a covering motion over the bottom man's upper body. He might hook his left arm over B's far ear and pull down and in on B's head, or he might block B's head down and catch under the far arm. A can force B's head away in a cross face action or hook B's near arm. All of these actions control B's upper body. A keeps constant chest pressure on B to restrict movement. A also controls B's near leg by lifting at the ankle or inside the thigh.

By aggressively pulling down and in on B's head and lifting up on the near leg, A drives his chest into B and forces him to a position on his stomach (Figure 13.2). This breakdown leads to the near-side cradle.

You should drill your wrestlers on the blanket ride until they can successfully cover the down man for 30 to 45 seconds. Start the drill by having the bottom man stay relatively motionless while the top man shifts hand position (Figure 13.1). Watch to see that the top wrestler lifts the near leg *at the same time* and that he hooks and controls B's head and upper body. As a more advanced drill, blow the whistle every 5 to 10 seconds as a signal for the bottom man to try to escape.

After your wrestlers have learned to control and break their opponents down with the blanket ride, you should teach them the near-side cradle. Teach your wrestlers not to rush through any of the techniques in this step. This is a series of controlled techniques that will help wrestlers score many near fall points and win more matches.

Figure 13.2. Blanket ride—breakdown.

NEAR-SIDE CRADLE

Most pins or near fall points are scored from either catching the opponent off balance or from a controlled position on the mat. The near-side cradle (Figure 13.3) is often executed with the defensive man on his hands and knees or hands and feet. The near-side cradle is a low-risk pinning combination that is successful even against skilled wrestlers. An aggressive move, this technique requires a fair degree of force and power. Proper position, in a way, compensates for lack of power, so wrestlers need to concentrate on the position of the arms and on the twisting motion.

Figure 13.3. Near-side cradle.

The top wrestler (A) uses a blanket ride to control an opponent on hands and knees. He spins B counterclockwise by pulling with his left elbow and lifting with his right arm. A has his right leg up in a tripod for increased power. A forces his hands together as he continues to spin. He slips his chest to a position on B's left side and locks his hands tightly as he forces B to his side on the mat. A secures near fall points or a pin by driving across B to a post position on his forehead. He keeps his hips up as he forces B to his back.

Sometimes the bottom wrestler raises his hips to a four-point stance on his hands and feet (Figure 13.4). If he does, the top wrestler can slip to the side and use a blanket ride. He can then drive his opponent to the mat with a near-side cradle as an offensive counter.

Figure 13.4. Near-side cradle from four-point stance.

Leg Traps

Often the near-side cradle can be applied from a position with the defensive man (B) on the mat. Sometimes the defensive man will counter the hold by dropping to the mat to prevent the top man (A) from lifting and spinning B to his back. The scoop and the basket (Figures 13.5 and 13.6, respectively) are techniques that involve leg-trapping motions that give the top man leverage. These moves really tie the bottom man up and almost always result in pins.

Scoop

A has a good cradle position, with B on the mat. He sits on his right hip and scoots his right knee under B's ankle. He then forces his left knee and hip under B's ankle. With a stepping motion toward B's head, A uses the lever of B's leg to drive him around and toward B's back. A completes the motion by planting his right knee on the mat near B's head. This action twists B's hips and turns him to his back.

Figure 13.5.   Scoop.

Basket

A lifts B's left leg at the knee as he forces B's head and shoulder down. He steps his right leg between B's legs and traps B's right ankle. Then, using his right leg, he drags B's ankle around while dropping his body over B's head. This pulling, twisting action puts B on his back. A has successfully turned B to a pinning position. B's legs are held down toward his head, forming a ''basket.''

Dumping the Opponent

Sometimes the defensive man will try to sit through to counter the near-side cradle. If he raises his head and shoulders, he can often break the lock that the offensive man has on his leg and neck. The top wrestler needs to expect this counter and be prepared to use it to his advantage.

Figure 13.6. Basket.

Figure 13.7. Dump with leg in.

Instead of trying to stop the sit-through motion, the offensive wrestler forces the opponent clear through and puts him on his back. Usually this technique results in near fall points, but not a pin. The top man can keep his near leg between B's legs (Figure 13.7) or move it to a position between their bodies (Figure 13.8).

The near-side cradle from the knees is a move that must be practiced. There is some danger involved in going up to the head or in getting too high over the bottom man. The defensive man needs to be controlled and kept off balance. The top man needs to use lifting pressure on the near leg and a hard bumping action to turn his opponent.

Figure 13.8. Dump with leg out.

TAKEDOWN COUNTERS

This step in the stairway to success is quite a broad one. These techniques are intended to first block the attacking man's attempts, then counter aggressively in a manner designed to score points. Some of the techniques incorporate portions of earlier skills; some are isolated skills. All of the counters assume that the opponent has started a leg attack series.

If a wrestler becomes skilled in these moves, he can bait the opponent into attempting a leg attack, then counter it aggressively.

These are techniques that you can easily teach to intermediate-level wrestlers. Some, such as the gut wrench (Figure 14.4) and the front quarter nelson (Figure 14.2), might even be taught at the beginning level. The block and drag, the elbow pancake, the arm shuck, and the front headlock, however, require changes of direction and a higher degree of body coordination.

HIGH-LEG COUNTER

The simplest counter to a takedown is to execute a good sprawl. Many times the offensive wrestler will still get hold of a leg if he has penetrated well. The defensive wrestler must then free that leg in order to have any chance of countering the takedown. The simplest moves are often the most effective. The high-leg counter (Figure 14.1) is simple, and it is effective because it exerts

Figure 14.1. High-leg counter.

a great deal of pressure right on top of the offensive man's shoulder. This action rips the defensive wrestler's leg free of the takedown man's grasp.

Wrestler B, on the right, has a single-leg, his hands locked on A's thigh. A keeps his hips down and his legs straight. A throws his right heel into the air in a high-leg arching motion; he forces his hips down while throwing his leg up. A frees his leg with hip motion and the tremendous power of his leg; in the extended position, B cannot hang on. A posts his right leg down and back as he starts to move behind B. A brings his right hand around for a cross face, completes the move, and goes behind for a takedown.

FRONT QUARTER NELSON

Success in the front quarter nelson (Figure 14.2) requires a quick, popping thrust with the hands to get the opponent's head down and away. The complete change of direction with both the head and the hips is the most difficult part of this technique. First, the wrestler must thrust in a clockwise direction. Once the opponent is posted on the mat, the wrestler must lift his head and rotate his hips in a counterclockwise direction. The first few times wrestlers try this move, they should do it slowly in order to understand the pressure points and the counterspin. Sometimes you may want to physically move the wrestler's body in the right direction so that he gets the feel of the movement.

Figure 14.2.   Front quarter nelson.

Wrestler A, on the left, has countered B's leg attack by using a good sprawl. He plants his right hand on the top of B's head, underhooks B's right arm, and grasps his own right wrist with his left hand. A forces B's head down with his hips. He pushes down hard on B's head with his right hand and forces up and forward with his left arm. A pops B's head away with a hard thrust with his hands. He drops his right shoulder to give added leverage. With B's head and left shoulder posted on the mat, A raises his head, moves his hips to the right, and underhooks B's head with his left hand. A has pulled his right hand out from under as he rotates. A hooks across B's body with his right elbow, forces with the left, and tries to come chest-to-chest with B, covering him with a reverse half nelson.

The front quarter nelson is very difficult to stop because there is so much pressure on the head. Therefore, it is one of the most effective counters to leg takedown attempts. The defensive wrestler should remember to sprawl hard first, then aggressively counter with the front quarter nelson.

ELBOW PANCAKE

The next takedown counter, the elbow pancake (Figure 14.3), is somewhat more difficult to teach, but once your wrestlers learn it, they will use it frequently because it puts the opponent on his back. The move is set up by pushing the takedown man's head down, then letting it pop

Figure 14.3. Elbow pancake.

up when he tries to raise it. The elbow pancake has a quick change of direction move that must almost be sensed.

Wrestler A, in the dark uniform, has countered B's double-leg tackle with a good sprawl. He posts his right hand on the top of B's head and forces it down into the mat. His left hand is caught loosely under B's right arm in an arm over-and-under position similar to that shown in the front quarter nelson (Figure 14.2). B lifts his head up; A lets it come up by releasing the pressure quickly. As B's head and shoulders come up, A rotates his forearm and elbow into B's forehead. A starts to drive in with his right hip as he begins a front to back motion. A uses B's upward and forward motion to pivot his body in the pancake action. A completes the move by shifting into a grip around the head and upper arm.

Wrestler A should not move his right hand off the head and try to come across the face. This action tips off the move, and speed and continuous motion are lost in the change of position with the arm.

This technique is really successful when used in conjunction with the front quarter nelson. After getting his head popped into the mat a few times in the front quarter nelson, Wrestler B will resist by jerking his head up. Then he is hit with an elbow pancake and put on his back. Either way he loses.

GUT WRENCH

The gut wrench is a very effective takedown counter if a wrestler has a good sprawl (Figure 14.4). He must get his legs back and get the opponent extended in double-leg tackle position.

Wrestler B, on the right, has executed a deep double-leg tackle. A pops his hips into B to stop B's forward motion, then controls B's head as he sprawls his legs back vigorously. As B tries to drive in from this position, he becomes extended with head and shoulders down. A reaches as far around the waist as he can get with a gut wrench position from the front. He pulls up in a twisting motion to throw B onto his side. A changes direction and covers B on the unprotected side. He forces his left elbow up into B's chest and underhooks B's head in a reverse nelson as he spins to cover.

Although the gut wrench may look like a simple move, there are a few key pressure points. Again, as in most of the more advanced techniques in wrestling, a complete change of direction is required. The arm action in the move also makes it work. First there is the gut wrench action; then the wrestler must use his elbows to hook B's arms and body as he moves around him, as shown in Figure 14.5.

OTHER COUNTERS

The takedown counters in this next set are used from a position where the attacker has not gotten in close enough to gain control of the hips or legs. The counter wrestler blocks and controls the head and one arm of the attacker. He can block and drag (Figure 14.6) or go to a front headlock position (Figure 14.7). From the front headlock he can use a near-side cradle to the near side (Figure 13.3) or an arm shuck (Figure 14.8).

Block and Drag

Wrestler A, in the dark uniform, keeps B from penetrating by blocking with his right elbow against B's shoulder (Figure 14.6). He controls B's right elbow. A pops his hand down and away as he cups his palm across the back of B's head and neck. He forces B's head away by extending his right arm thumb-down. He pulls B's body across in front with a short drag on the right

Figure 14.4. Sprawl to gut wrench.

Figure 14.5. Elbow hook.

elbow. Completing the move, A goes behind for a takedown. This move uses B's driving momentum and simply whips his head on by.

Figure 14.6. Block and drag.

Front Headlock and Go-Behind

Wrestler A, in the light uniform, blocks B's takedown attempt with his sprawl (Figure 14.7). His right biceps is against B's left shoulder; his left forearm forces B's right arm in and forward.

Figure 14.7. Front headlock and go-behind.

A locks his hands around B's head and right arm. A's left palm is turned up in the lock so that his left elbow is forced in and forward. He extends B's body by pulling with the lock. His head must be posted low and tight in B's side. A keeps B's head down and arm controlled with his right hand. He moves to the side as he reaches for B's leg. A completes the move by slipping behind. From there he can use a near-side cradle (Figure 13.3).

Arm Shuck

As the wrestler tries to use the front headlock to cradle, the defensive man will usually spin to stay square in a facing position. This motion sets up the arm shuck (Figure 14.8). The most important motion is the upward jabbing action of A's right arm, as illustrated in the last two photos.

Figure 14.8.   Arm shuck from front headlock.

ADVANCED WRESTLING SKILLS

The skills illustrated in this stage of *Successful Wrestling* are intended for wrestlers who have had 2 or 3 years of experience. Many of these techniques require a high level of body coordination and agility. In addition, their successful execution depends upon a well-established "mat sense." Skilled wrestlers must possess the feel for when a move can be executed; they must have the sense of timing that is often the difference between success and failure.

Wrestlers can achieve a high level of success even without knowing any of the moves illustrated in this stage. Championship wrestlers primarily execute the fundamentals effectively, and most of them do not possess a wide variety of skills but are highly skilled in a few moves.

Stage 3 begins with more takedowns. Leg rides for control and for pinning follow. "Take-down Options," step 17, shows methods of combining several takedowns and of changing from one takedown to another. Takedowns designed for special situations are included in step 18. These are especially effective techniques for heavier wrestlers.

The last step in this stage demonstrates the importance of analyzing, drilling, and sequencing wrestling technique. Wrestling is a highly complex sport; there is almost an infinite number of possible combinations. You will need to make some choices about the number of techniques and the learning progression for your program. The illustrations included in step 19 are intended to give direction to that sorting-out process.

MORE TAKEDOWNS

Previous takedowns have used a straight-in penetration to both legs, as in the double-leg tackle or a right-hand attack to the opponent's left leg in the outside fireman's carry and the single-leg attack. All three takedowns emphasized the importance of penetration and changing levels with the hips. In the double-leg tackle, both arms of the attacking wrestler were shot past and outside the defensive man's hips. In the outside fireman's carry, the right arm went outside and the left controlled the right arm of the opponent. The single-leg attack was performed with the right arm outside and the left inside.

The two takedowns demonstrated in this step—the fireman's carry and the high-crotch single—use a deep penetrating action with the right hand and shoulder between the defensive man's legs. The action of the right arm is in and up, rather than around the legs, in both takedowns.

Furthermore, both takedowns are demonstrated from the staggered stance, and both begin with the inside tie-up that has been emphasized repeatedly. These two new techniques are highly effective, but they require a slightly higher level of coordination. The attacking wrestler must change direction in each of these moves.

FIREMAN'S CARRY

The fireman's carry is an excellent move because it often leads directly to near fall points as the defensive man is put on his back from the standing position. This technique requires a twisting motion in under the opponent and involves ''carrying'' the man over the attacking wrestler's shoulders. The fireman's carry starts with the staggered stance and an elbow hook. You should teach your wrestlers to begin all takedowns from a similar stance and tie so that the opponent does not know which technique will follow.

The fireman's carry requires the attacking wrestler to get the defensive man's upper body motion forward (Figure 15.1). In order to do this, he must have a good grip on one arm of the opponent. Sometimes the move can be set up by pushing against the defensive wrestler until he resists by pushing back.

Wrestler A (light uniform) drops his hips as he begins his penetration. He steps forward with his right foot and extends his right arm through B's legs. His head must get under B's arm. A whips his right side into B as he comes to both knees with a 90° turn. A clamps B's right arm down tightly and thrusts his right upper arm high into B's hip area. A pivots his left knee and tucks his left foot under him, then extends his right foot between B's feet: These foot rotations are done simultaneously by pivoting on the knees. A vigorously posts his left side to the mat, carrying B's head and shoulders down. A drives his right arm up and through B's body as he continues to sit through. A keeps B's shoulders posted on the mat while stepping through with his right leg, continuing the twisting motion with his body and hips to a sit-through pancake position for near fall points.

Figure 15.1. Fireman's carry.

The foot rotation is an important part of this technique. The attacking wrestler lands on both knees, with his feet trailing his knees. He must then swivel so that the feet are in advance of his knees in order to change direction (Figure 15.2). This technique should be practiced both without a partner and with a partner.

The main goal of this technique is to get the defensive man's upper body moving in a straight line over the top of the attacker's knees. Often wrestlers grasp the leg incorrectly at the knee (Figure 15.3a). From that position, lifting becomes quite difficult. Furthermore, the opponent should not be dumped on his side over the attacker's head (Figure 15.3b) but should be carried over the offensive man's shoulder and dumped onto his own head.

The fireman's carry requires a deep penetration of the right shoulder and arm. Therefore, for greatest success the attacking wrestler must get the defensive man's upper body moving in. The offensive man may push with his right arm so that his opponent pushes back, or the attacking wrestler may retreat a step or two to get the other man to pursue.

A key coaching point for this move is that the takedown man cannot simply drop to his knees; he must drive in hard with knee, arm, and shoulder.

Figure 15.2. Foot position.

Figure 15.3. Incorrect positions.

Barrel Roll

Sometimes the offensive wrestler is unable to get in deep with his right arm. If he cannot get in far enough to carry the opponent onto his shoulders, he may need to follow through with a second move. The barrel roll (Figure 15.4) completes the fireman's carry action against a man who has sprawled his weight back.

Wrestler B, on the left, has sprawled his legs back and dropped his hips, keeping A from penetrating to get his right arm in deep enough to get the carry position necessary for a successful fireman's carry. A keeps B's right arm clamped tightly. He posts his right hand on the mat and gets shoulder elevation by extending his arm. A dumps his head and left shoulder to the mat as he sits through with his left leg and thrusts his right arm across B's waist. A continues the

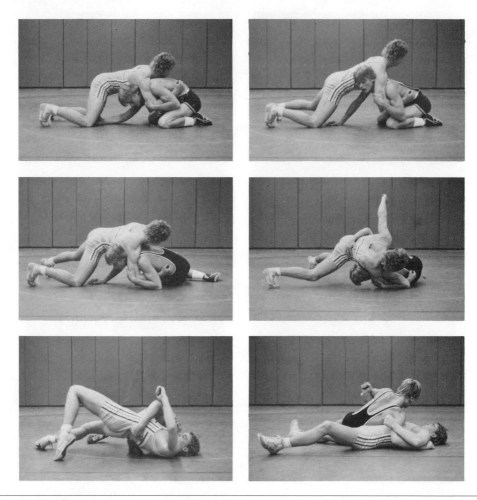

Figure 15.4.   Barrel roll.

hip motion as he turns B's shoulders to the mat; he must pull his head up as he rotates to complete the move in near fall position.

Because the defensive man's body is extended, he has no braces to stop the barrel roll. The attacking wrestler can set up this move by continuing to crawl into the defensive man, who will probably stretch out further. As he extends his legs behind, he becomes as easy to roll over as a barrel.

Underarm Spin

The underarm spin (Figure 15.5) works well against a wrestler who has countered with a good sprawl. The underarm spin uses a lifting, spinning motion to secure a takedown without the carry motion.

Wrestler A, in the dark uniform, drives up into B. He must keep B from underhooking the right arm as he slides his right arm and shoulder through and starts a hip heist motion. A keeps his head up and pivots under B's arm. He must scoot clear of B's weight. He drives B to the mat with head and shoulder pressure as he completes the spin and covers B.

Figure 15.5. Underarm spin.

Shift to Double-Leg Tackle

Another follow-up move that may be used if the attacking wrestler cannot penetrate deep enough is a shift to a double-leg tackle (Figure 2.1). To shift, the attacking wrestler removes his hand from between the legs and moves to a double-leg tackle position with his right arm (Figure 15.6).

Double-Arm Underhook to Double-Leg Tackle

If the attacking wrestler does not get his right shoulder turned in and a 90° turn with his body, he may end up on both knees under his opponent's sprawl. The opponent may even underhook the other arm so that he has a defensive double-arm underhook. If the attacking wrestler finds himself caught in this position, he should stay square with his shoulders and stand up into the defensive wrestler (Figure 15.7). Once he reaches his feet, the offensive wrestler vigorously drops his hips and legs in as he forces his hands forward to a double-leg tackle position. The sudden drop and penetration is an unexpected move. The defending wrestler is depending on his double underhook to counter, but the forward motion of Wrestler A completely overpowers the counter.

Figure 15.6. Shift to double-leg tackle.

Figure 15.7. Double-arm underhook to double-leg tackle.

HIGH-CROTCH SINGLE

The high-crotch single (Figure 15.8) is a leg attack that is extremely effective. It will work against very good opponents and is hard to counter. The attacking man gets deep penetration and prevents the opponent from sprawling his weight back. The move is completed in a lift that takes the defensive man off his supports.

As with all the takedowns shown in this book, the high-crotch single starts with the inside tie-up on the elbow and with a staggered stance. As the offensive man starts his move, it looks much like the fireman's carry and many other takedowns, so the defensive wrestler does not expect it. The attacking wrestler can go to his knee in his penetration, or he can step in with a quick change of level in order to get under the defending wrestler's arms.

The most powerful advantage for this technique against good wrestlers is that the offensive wrestler is attacking only one leg. He is attacking it at the hip joint, so he does not have to fight the powerful thigh muscles. Additionally, he attacks with the pivoting action to the side, which avoids his being trapped under the defensive man's weight in a sprawl.

A (on the right) sets up the move by pulling down sharply on B's upper arm, then lifts B's right arm and begins his penetration. A shoots his right knee between B's legs, drops his hips down and forward, and thrusts his right arm high inside B's crotch. A begins to come up with his right arm and his hips; he does not drop in with the 90° body twist of the fireman's carry. A releases B's arm and thrusts his left hand around and deep in B's crotch while stepping forward and around with his left foot. A continues to pivot with his hips as he stands up. He has B's right thigh grasped high in the crotch; his hips are in tight at B's thigh.

Figure 15.8. High-crotch single.

Setups

Alternate positions of the left hand at the start can be used to set up successful completion of the high-crotch single. Three of these hand positions are shown in the next series (Figure 15.9). The first setup is shown out of an inside tie-up. The opponent's arm is pulled forward and down. As the opponent tries to lift his arm, the attacker releases and starts his move. Sometimes the inside-out tie on the elbow is hard to get because the defensive man uses a collar tie, which is hard to get inside. In that case, the attacking wrestler overhooks the elbow from the outside, pulls down hard, then releases as he penetrates. A simple alternative to the overhook is for the attacking man to grasp the elbow, push it in, and release.

Figure 15.9.   Setups.

Lift

The high-crotch single requires a fair degree of quickness and agility. The rapid penetration with the right side of the body is followed by a pivot to the left. This change of direction is necessary in order to lift. The lifting motion for this technique is accompanied by a change of hand position and a continuation of the clockwise pivot with the hips. The attacking wrestler works from the side of his opponent to neutralize counters and to get hip action into the lift (Figure 15.10).

The return to the mat action required at the end of the high-crotch single is much like the techniques used to return the man to the mat after a stand-up (Figure 4.5). You should emphasize these similarities so that your wrestlers recognize various positions for each technique. As they become fluid and coordinated, they become more versatile and successful. They will even develop their own variations.

The similarity of the starting positions of the fireman's carry and the high-crotch single should also be emphasized. Often a wrestler can start the penetration action and take whichever move seems to be easier to complete, given the reaction of the defensive man. The setups shown here are equally appropriate for the duck-under (step 18) and the double-leg tackle (step 2). Some-

Figure 15.10.   Lift.

times the defensive wrestler successfully counters the first penetrating action of the attacking wrestler by keeping his right leg back and his body square. In this case, the offensive man shifts to a double-leg tackle. He can use the same setup and the same lifts once he gets penetration.

Standing High-Crotch Single

Some wrestlers do not like to go to their knees on takedowns. The standing high-crotch single (Figure 15.11) is an excellent technique in this situation if the offensive man is quick and has a good change of level with his upper body. The movement is much like the duck-under (Figure 18.1) in that the wrestler must get in and under the arm of the defensive man. He does this by using one of the setups effectively.

Figure 15.11.   High-crotch without going to knees.

STEP 16

LEG RIDES

In step 10 the turk ride was shown as a pinning hold from a position on the mat when the defensive wrestler had already been broken down to his stomach. This step will now illustrate more advanced techniques for controlling and pinning a wrestler using leg rides.

Of all the moves in wrestling, leg rides are probably incorrectly taught more frequently than any other skill. Two basic improper positions make the leg rides somewhat risky. The first is when the top man stays parallel instead of using a cross-body ride or riding at nearly a 90° angle. The second fault is when the top man puts his leg in too far and then cannot exert good pressure; he ends up just hanging on and not turning his opponent. To avoid these two errors, the basic positions and techniques shown in Figures 10.6 through 10.9 should be reviewed.

Wrestlers who have learned how to use the turk ride from a flat position should have no problem with the more advanced skills shown in this step. Several variations are included here; all are effective as pinning combinations and should be practiced with the idea of turning the opponent to his back. A wrestler should not be content to merely control his man, but should exert pressure and score points or secure a pin.

Few wrestlers spend the time necessary to become proficient in either using or countering leg rides. Therefore, wrestlers who do become skilled in leg rides will find they have a decided advantage over their opponents.

CROSS-BODY RIDE

The cross-body ride series has many options. Once a wrestler learns how to apply the force correctly, he will be able to score near fall points or secure a pin. The leg rides are excellent for controlling the bottom man. Unfortunately, most referees break the hold by calling either stalling or a stalemate unless the top man has created a pinning situation.

The top wrestler must be aggressive and apply a great deal of twisting force with his legs in order to improve the leg rides from merely controlling to turning the bottom man. The key to the cross-body ride series rests in the proper leg and knee placement. A second factor that is important is to establish body position across the wrestler's lower back rather than a parallel position. Because these positions are so important for success, these techniques are illustrated in the first series.

Cross-Body Ride From Knees

Wrestler A starts the cross-body ride (Figure 16.1) from a blanket ride. He controls B's head with pressure from his left arm. A grasps B's far ankle to stop his motion. A extends his body up high and across the small of B's back. He holds the far ankle as an anchor. His left hipbone is up over B's back. A puts his left lower leg inside B's left knee; he does not hook B's lower leg with his toe. A rotates his hip down and his knee to the outside. This pressure breaks B

Figure 16.1. Cross-body ride from knees.

down to his stomach. A is driving forward with his right leg and lifting up on B's right ankle to get additional force. A turns B's hips over by lifting his left knee up and rotating his hips down to the right. A great deal of pressure is exerted if this motion is done correctly.

The top wrestler often sticks his leg in too far, which keeps his hips too low and prevents him from getting up across B's back (Figure 16.2a). Figure 16.2b shows the correct position, with his leg in just enough to hook it inside B's knee. A has his left knee forward and rotated out, with his body up and across B's back.

Figure 16.2. Leg position incorrect/correct.

Cross-Body Ride Counter

The defensive wrestler's best counter to the cross-body ride series is motion preventing the top man from getting his leg hooked in. However, if the top man does get his leg in and hooked, the bottom man should try to neutralize the leg action first, then turn in to free his own leg (Figure 16.3).

Figure 16.3. Post and heist counter.

The top wrestler (B) has a fairly good cross-body ride position. The defensive man (A) clamps B's left knee down and in, using his left hand. A whips his left hip to the mat and gets B off the across-the-back position necessary for B's success; A must post his hip down hard and keep his left side turned down to the mat. A scoots his hips back and underhooks B's left knee with his right hand. He keeps his right elbow down to protect it and continues to scoot down and away from B. A uses a hip heist motion to clear his hips and force B to his back. He completes the leg-lift action and the hip heist motion to secure a reversal and put B in trouble.

FORCE NELSON

If the defensive wrestler is not successful in the above counter, the top man may work for a force nelson (Figure 16.4). The offensive wrestler can also put on the force nelson when he has a leg ride and the defensive man tries to stay flat on the mat.

Wrestler A (on top) has not been able to turn B's hips. This position may occur as B tries to block the leg ride with the post and heist counter (Figure 16.3). A posts his left elbow on the

Figure 16.4. Force nelson.

back of B's head and reaches under B's right arm with his own right to lock his hands. He grasps his own wrist for maximum leverage and, using both arms, forces B's head down and away. He keeps the leg hook for control. A extends his right arm to force B's head away, and hooks B's right arm with his left as he twists B to an exposed position. A gets maximum pressure with his right arm by rotating his thumb down and away.

Force Nelson From Double-Leg Ride

The top wrestler (A) is in a good cross-body ride, but the bottom man has a wide, stable base (Figure 16.5). A plants his left forearm at the base of B's skull and steps his right leg across and inside B's legs for a double-leg ride. A uses a force nelson, with his left palm up in the grip for increased pressure. He drives down with his hips and up with his heels. A forces B to the mat; by pushing hard with both hands on B's head and continuing the double-leg ride pressure, A turns B onto his back. He can secure the pin by forcing down on B's right arm and extending his right hand behind B's head.

Figure 16.5.   Force nelson from double-leg ride.

ARM HOOK

Sometimes the bottom man tries to counter the force nelson or double-leg ride by sitting through with his far leg. When he does, the top man catches his arm with an overhook and drops him back using arm and leg pressure (Figure 16.6). This arm hook is an easy move to learn if the top man stays close and keeps pressure with the leg ride. He actually crowds into B as he catches the arm.

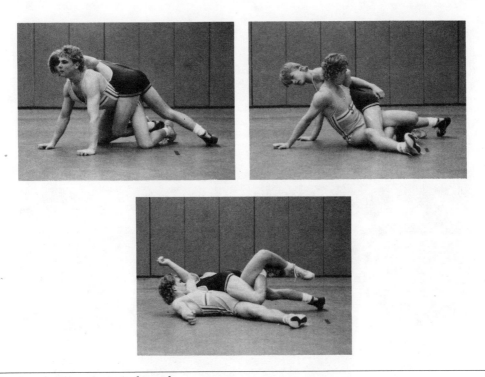

Figure 16.6. Arm hook against sit-through.

GUILLOTINE

The guillotine gets its name because of its pressure on the neck. When the top man executes the cross-body ride and then hooks the head in the manner shown (Figure 16.7), he has exposed his opponent's shoulders to the mat. Properly done, the move can be aptly described as "taking the man's head off."

Actually, the most likely physical damage to the defensive man would occur in the shoulder area. The defender's arm must be slowly pulled across the body rather than forward. The guillotine does leave the opponent rather helpless and as vulnerable as the ancient French guillotine.

The top man underhooks B's right arm at the elbow. He has his body well across B's back and a good leg hook with his left knee rotating out. A pulls up on B's arm while forcing down with his hips and rotating his left knee out to break down B's hip braces. A grasps B's right wrist and keeps B's arm straight. A extends his head and left shoulder under B's arm as he controls the arm at the wrist. Because this position is potentially dangerous, A must be careful not to jerk the arm toward B's head and cause injury. A overhooks B's head with his left arm while reaching across B's chest with his right arm. He completes a guillotine by grasping B's head with his right arm and forcing B's shoulders to the mat for a pin.

TURK RIDE FROM KNEES

Once wrestlers have learned the pressure points for the turk ride while controlling a flat man (Figure 10.6), they are ready to work on the technique when the defensive man is on his hands

Figure 16.7.   Guillotine.

and knees (Figure 16.8). The top wrestler must break the man down to the mat before he can complete the turk ride. He gets the breakdown by stretching the defensive wrestler and turning his hips with the turk ride.

The top wrestler (A) has a good cross-body ride. He reaches across to B's far wrist and straightens it out while using leg pressure to break the defensive man down to his stomach. From there he can turn the man with the turk ride.

The leg rides shown in this step require much practice. The best drills are really to have your wrestlers practice a series of situations. Have your wrestlers put on a cross-body ride in the starting position. Then have the bottom man try to escape as the top man works any of the techniques—guillotine, turk, or force nelson. A great deal of just rolling around with the legs hooked in provides the best practice. Also, rather than work on isolated drills, your wrestlers can use the concept of a scramble. The hold is put on by one man, then both scramble to execute the hold or a counter.

Figure 16.8. Breakdown from knees.

STEP 17

TAKEDOWN OPTIONS

This step illustrates choices a wrestler must make in executing takedowns. Superior wrestlers have mastered a few techniques so well that they can score on most opponents using these special skills. However, often one move will lead to the defensive man's counter, which opens up possibilities for the attacker's use of another move.

FOLLOW-UP MOVES FROM A DOUBLE-LEG TACKLE

The double-leg tackle is such a basic part of wrestling that it was taught as part of the first technique in step 2. Sometimes the defensive man counters in such a way that the takedown can be gained more easily by shifting from the double-leg tackle to an alternative such as a single-leg attack or the submarine.

Double to Single

Wrestler A, on the left in Figure 17.1, penetrates on a double-leg tackle. B counters with a sprawl and shifts his weight to his left leg. A changes direction and shifts to a single-leg attack against B's left leg. He drives up and in as he now works at the single-leg, instead of the double-leg he had started.

Figure 17.1. Double to single.

Double to Submarine

Wrestler A starts a double-leg tackle while B executes a good sprawl and forces A's head down (Figure 17.2). A posts his left hand on the mat, straightens his left arm, and lifts with his head in B's crotch. He penetrates with his left knee, lifting B's hips. A posts his left hand under B's right leg. A throws B's leg away and pulls down with his right hand as he spins through to gain the takedown.

Figure 17.2.   Double to submarine.

PINNING FROM THE TAKEDOWN

Successful wrestlers must constantly look for back points and the pin from all positions. When the competition reaches its highest level, the wrestler should turn his opponent anytime he can. Really good opportunities for the aggressive wrestler are presented off the double-leg tackle. Three are now shown, the first two requiring the wrestler to pick up his opponent in the double-leg.

Double-Leg Pick Up and Spin

Wrestler A penetrates deep with a good drop of his hips (Figure 17.3); he does not touch his knees to the mat. With explosive motion he lifts B from the mat. A swings B's legs across his chest, using his right forearm against the outside of B's thigh. He underhooks B's right thigh with his left arm. A drops to his right knee as he spins B's legs across his front. A blocks B's legs with his left thigh as he pulls his right arm out. He drives B's shoulders to the mat and shoots in a half nelson with his right arm while keeping B's legs trapped. By driving into B's chest, A can secure a pin with the half nelson.

Figure 17.3. Double-leg pick up and spin.

Inside Turk

An agile wrestler with good balance can put the inside turk on his opponent as they go to the mat. In Figure 17.4 the attacking wrestler has penetrated deep with a good level change and

Figure 17.4. Inside turk to a near fall.

has lifted B from the mat. While driving forward and down, he steps between B's legs, his left heel catching behind B's left leg. He puts his opponent on the mat in near fall position.

Half Nelson From Double-Leg Tackle

Anytime the attacking wrestler puts his opponent on the mat, he should be looking for an opportunity to pin his opponent. Many times a half nelson is easily secured when the defensive man is put on the mat out of the double-leg tackle (Figure 17.5).

Figure 17.5. Half nelson from double-leg tackle.

ADDITIONAL COMBINATIONS

Coaches and wrestlers who have reached this ''Advanced Wrestling Skills'' stage will be able to put many moves together. An example of another combination, the left-hand thrust, is shown in Figure 17.6. The attacking wrestler (A) has started either a high-crotch single or a fireman's carry. The defender has used a good sprawl to counter, trapping the attacker down to the mat. A quick thrust forward with A's left hand to his opponent's ankle will square A up and allow him to score a takedown with a modification of the double-leg tackle.

Many more combinations are possible. Only enough have been illustrated in this step to hint at the concept of going from one move to another. As your wrestlers gain skill, you should have them practice putting moves together in sequence. The champion knows what techniques he is attempting and what he will do next. Many matches between skilled wrestlers are won by the man who skillfully completes a chain of maneuvers, one following another as a scramble unfolds.

Figure 17.6. Left-hand thrust.

STEP 18

SPECIALTY TAKEDOWNS

This step illustrates five takedowns that increase a wrestler's versatility. They are placed in this "Advanced Wrestling Skills" section because they are not essential for initial success. Each is a separate move; each is executed out of the basic stance and tie.

These five takedowns are good moves for heavyweights and probably should be taught earlier for such wrestlers. The wrestler neither goes to his knees nor gets the opponent's weight on him in these takedowns.

Two duck-under moves are shown. Some wrestlers will find that one feels more natural than the other; they should develop skill in the preferred one. Each results in a rear or side standing position from which a standing breakdown (step 4) is used. Next, the standing shuck and the short drag both use hand and arm action for getting behind the opponent. The arm drag to double-leg is a combination of the short drag and the double-leg tackle (step 2). Quickness is necessary in the first stages of this technique, but once the move is started, it is difficult to counter.

DUCK-UNDER

The regular duck-under (Figure 18.1) begins from the staggered stance with inside tie-up. The aggressive wrestler pushes hard on his opponent's shoulders and upper body as he tries to get the opponent to push back. Then, as the name suggests, the wrestler ducks his head under his opponent's arm.

Figure 18.1. Duck-under.

Wrestler A, in the dark uniform, pushes hard in the inside tie-up in order to get resistance. A drops his hips, steps in quickly, and punches his head under B's right arm. He gets body penetration by stepping with his right foot. A steps around with his left foot while pivoting on his right, and gets his hips in tight for control.

Pull and Duck-Under

In Figure 18.2, the wrestlers are in a conventional tie-up. A (dark uniform) jerks B's head and left side down and forward with the right hand. He pops B's right elbow up and steps forward and around with his left foot. He drops his hips and executes the duck-under. A comes to a side standing position. He must take B to the mat for control.

Figure 18.2.   Pull and duck-under.

DRAG VARIATIONS

Several techniques use either a snapping drag or a shuck to slip past the opponent. One example that used the forward momentum of the other wrestler was the arm shuck (Figure 14.8). The attacking wrestler forces in on the shoulder and/or head of his opponent. As the other man resists, the wrestler snaps, or shucks, him by and goes to a controlling position behind or to the side.

Standing Shuck

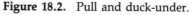

The standing shuck (Figure 18.3) works well against a wrestler who stays in close with a tie-up and pushes.

The wrestlers are in a tight tie-up. A (dark uniform) grasps B's right elbow with his palm up and squeezes with his thumb. He reaches across with his right hand in a feint to B's right leg. B reacts by jerking it back. A has an underhook on B's elbow with his right hand; he snaps his left across the back of B's neck and shoulders as he pivots on his right foot. A continues the pivot to shuck B by with powerful arm movements. He now can go behind.

The standing shuck is particularly effective after several leg attack attempts. The defensive wrestler tries to counter by getting a tight tie-up and by hanging on. He is also conscious of his legs and reacts when the aggressor fakes at his leg.

Figure 18.3. Standing shuck.

Arm Drags

Two arm drag techniques are particularly good moves for heavyweight wrestlers. Each technique relies on a quick hooking motion with the hands to drag the body of the defensive wrestler (light uniform) in close. He will react by drawing back and planting his feet. The attacking wrestler (A) then either pivots around B in the short drag (Figure 18.4) or hits him with a double-leg

Figure 18.4. Short drag.

tackle (Figure 18.5). The arm drag to double-leg is an excellent technique because it is so hard to counter. It does, however, require quickness, an aggressive pop with the chest, and good hand coordination.

Figure 18.5.   Arm drag to double-leg tackle.

STEP 19

COACHING POINTS

As a coach, you need to learn, then teach your wrestlers, coaching points for the various techniques. These coaching points are the little but important details, such as angle of the foot and placement of a hand with the palm up instead of down. From the first day in the practice room, you must teach the correct positions and proper motions. Success in wrestling requires attention to detail.

Successful coaches must be able to analyze a technique to discover its coaching points, be able to develop drills to help wrestlers become proficient, and be able to put a series of individual moves into coordinated chains of action. This step offers suggestions and illustrations for more successful coaching.

ANALYZING A TECHNIQUE

Each of the technique discussions included in this book is based on an analysis of the required body position and the physical development level of the athlete. This concept is illustrated by the use of the staggered stance and inside tie-up. The decision to use only one stance and one tie-up throughout the book was based on a careful analysis of the choices. The inside tie-up provides an easily learned hand and arm placement. It offers definite counter advantage. Most of all, though, it is an aggressive control position. Once a wrestler has learned the tie-up, he can concentrate on takedown penetration.

Because all of the takedowns are executed from the same stance and tie-up, the opponent does not know which attack will be used. This simplicity adds deception to the advantage of a comfortable, automatic position on the feet. Figure 19.1 illustrates the similarity among the takedowns used in this book.

Wrestler A (light uniform) starts with a staggered stance and an inside tie-up. He then penetrates for a double-leg tackle. Next he uses the knee outside and an elbow hook for the outside fireman's carry. Then he is shown hitting the single-leg attack, penetrating between B's legs in a fireman's carry, and changing position slightly as he plants a high-crotch single. He finishes with a simple duck-under.

By keeping the same stance and tie-up, wrestlers can concentrate on the execution of several following moves. The similarity of moves shown in Figure 19.1 is the result of a careful analysis of takedowns. Although the square stance may have advantages for some wrestlers and some situations, the benefits of a single stance and tie-up seem superior.

Coaches and wrestlers are encouraged to conduct their own analysis of a number of techniques.

Another deliberate integration used in this book is further proof of the benefits of analyzing the coaching points of individual moves and the similarities between moves. For example, the hip heist was first introduced in Figure 1.22. Throughout the rest of the book, the hip heist is shown as part of a great many moves, such as the inside and outside stand-ups and the switch away.

Figure 19.1.   Analyzing takedowns.

DRILLING FOR SKILL

Successful wrestlers perform a great many movements as natural reactions to positions or situations. You must have wrestlers practice these moves repeatedly as both solo and partner drills so that habitual response occurs.

Because practice time is normally limited, use the warm-up time to drill moves. Emphasis on correct position and movement should come first; then shift to speed, power, and endurance. Additional benefit can be gained from using these drills as cardiovascular or stretching activities. Increased flexibility and coordination are also important outcomes. A set of 30 or even 50 jumping jacks does not do a wrestler much good, but a drill of 30 seconds' worth of hip heists will develop coordination and stretch the legs, back, and arms, all while developing a valuable wrestling skill.

CHAINING A SERIES OF MOVES

One of the most noticeable characteristics of highly successful wrestlers is their ability to hit a sequence of moves. They seem to go through a scramble and end up in control. No sequence of moves is predetermined, though. Rather, a wrestler starts a move, which his opponent counters. He counters the counter, and a flurry of activity results, with one wrestler emerging victorious. The skill of quickly using optimum counters in a chain can and should be part of wrestling practice.

As soon as you have taught two moves, you should start teaching ways to use the moves in succession. This concept is easily demonstrated: In step 1, the beginning wrestler learned the knee scoot (Figure 1.17) and the hip heist (Figure 1.22); at that point, the wrestlers should start practicing the moves in a chain of continuous motion, such as shown in Figure 19.2.

The solo wrestler scoots his right knee forward and raises his head and shoulders from the bottom position. He simulates being forced back to his hands and knees. Without hesitation,

Figure 19.2. Knee scoot to hip heist.

he hops forward to post right foot and left hand. He sits through with his left foot and posts his left foot and right hand. He completes the hip heist and prepares to start back the other way.

Figure 19.3 shows a drill that combines four techniques—the sit-out, the duck-out, the power switch, and the hip heist. This is a drill you should have wrestlers practice as a warm-up activity every practice session. The wrestler does a short sit-out, then drops his head and shoulder in a duck-out. With a rapid change of direction, the wrestler starts a power switch, finishes with a hip heist, then pushes back with his hands to regain a starting position, ready to hit another move.

A successful wrestling program is characterized by wrestlers and coaches who take the time to analyze, drill, and chain the various techniques. Wrestling is such an exciting sport to participate in because one can never learn all there is to know. Hopefully, you have caught some of this excitement and will be inspired to continue to develop yourself and your team.

Figure 19.3. Drilling mat moves.